10638188

The New York Times

WILL SHORTZ PRESENTS I LOVE CROSSWORDS

From the Pages of *The New York Times*

Edited by Will Shortz

ST. MARTIN'S GRIFFIN ✿ NEW YORK

THE NEW YORK TIMES WILL SHORTZ PRESENTS I LOVE CROSSWORDS.
Copyright © 2007 by The New York Times Company. All rights reserved.
Printed in the United States of America. No part of this book may be
used or reproduced in any manner whatsoever without written
permission except in the case of brief quotations embodied
in critical articles or reviews. For information, address
St. Martin's Press, 175 Fifth Avenue, New York, NY 10010.

www.stmartins.com

All of the puzzles that appear in this work were originally published
in *The New York Times* from June 28, 2004, to September 22, 2004.
Copyright © 2004 by The New York Times Company.
All Rights Reserved. Reprinted by permission.

ISBN-13: 978-0-312-37040-4
ISBN-10: 0-312-37040-7

10 9 8 7 6 5 4 3 2

The New York Times

WILL SHORTZ PRESENTS I LOVE CROSSWORDS

ACROSS

1 Crossword pattern
5 Dinner and a movie, perhaps
9 No longer fresh
14 Prefix with space
15 Sharif of "Funny Girl"
16 Swatch competitor
17 Convention group
18 Sitarist Shankar
19 Christopher of "Superman"
20 Polyester, e.g.
23 Battering device
24 Words before tear or roll
25 Astroturf, e.g.
34 Everest or Ararat
35 Comic strip orphan
36 Country singer Brenda
37 Johnson of "Laugh-In"
38 Vision-related
39 Darn, as socks
40 Lunar New Year
41 Grand Canyon transport
42 Contemptible person
43 Oleomargarine, e.g.
46 Airport monitor abbr.
47 Blonde shade
48 Fake 50, e.g.
57 Throng
58 Banjo-plucking Scruggs
59 Hand lotion ingredient
60 Indy-winning Al, Jr. or Sr.
61 Canal of song
62 It's trapped on laundry day
63 Sirs' counterparts
64 Give temporarily
65 Falls behind

DOWN

1 Chews the fat
2 Depend (on)
3 "Pumping ___"
4 Marxism, for one
5 Starting notes in music
6 Amo, amas, ___ . . .
7 Rikki-Tikki-___
8 Guitarist Clapton
9 Eerie
10 Item of men's jewelry
11 From the United States: Abbr.
12 Jeans purveyor Strauss
13 Business V.I.P.
21 Sword handle
22 ___ acid (B vitamin)
25 Maker of precious violins
26 Composer/author Ned
27 ___-frutti
28 Isle in the Bay of Naples
29 Emcee's spiel
30 Negatively charged particle
31 Alaskan native
32 "Common" thing that's not always common
33 Passover feast
38 Bizarre
39 Closet larvae repellent
41 Does deals without money
42 Earthy desire
44 Bicycle for two
45 Tried to save a sinking boat
48 Buddy
49 One of the O'Neills
50 ___ Major
51 Rod's partner
52 Price of a ride
53 "___ go bragh"
54 Pelvic bones
55 Beyond the end line
56 Answer to "Shall we?"

by Sarah Keller

2

ACROSS

1 Opportunity to hit
6 Shoots 18, say
11 Rocks in a bar
14 Long green
15 The Beatles' "Eight Days ___"
16 Turf
17 Result of eating ice cream too fast, possibly
19 Moth-eaten
20 Best guess: Abbr.
21 Fastens with a band
22 "That is ___ . . ." (in other words)
24 Town next to Elizabeth, N.J.
26 Flexible, electrically
27 Fondue dip
32 Bops hard
35 Light as a feather
36 Pot's top
37 Spa wear
38 En ___ (all together)
40 Place for a ham
41 Where Schwarzenegger was born: Abbr.
42 "Lost our lease" event
43 Airplane seating option
44 Entreater's words
48 Asta's mistress
49 The whole ___ (everything)
53 Must, slangily
55 Debaters debate it
57 Shaq's alma mater: Abbr.
58 Copy
59 Sunshine State vacation area
62 Snore letter
63 3 on a par-5 hole, e.g.
64 Largish combo
65 Golfer Ernie
66 Collar inserts
67 Quaint footwear

DOWN

1 Color of waves of grain, in song
2 Sculpted figure
3 Bath toys
4 2001 role for Will Smith
5 Comb stoppers
6 Attic
7 Was in the red
8 Dregs
9 Shriner's topper
10 Missing many details
11 Kind of triangle
12 RC, for one
13 Whirling water
18 "___ 'er up!"
23 Pindar work
25 One-named supermodel
26 Plot unit
28 Studio prop
29 Insult, slangily
30 Spot for a warm pie
31 Falco of "The Sopranos"
32 Shawl or stole
33 Billing unit
34 Some voters
38 Yucatán native
39 Gran Paradiso, for one
40 Per ___
42 Attacks from the air
43 Sub sinkers, in slang
45 Young 'un
46 Catches sight of
47 Like gastric juice
50 Dementieva of tennis
51 So far
52 Corrodes
53 Stare intently
54 Kadett automaker
55 Fraternity party attire
56 Paris airport
60 Long. crosser
61 Keystone lawman

by Jim Hyres

ACROSS

1 "Hardball" channel
6 Tim of "WKRP"
10 Actor McGregor
14 Car hitch-up
15 Best of theater
16 Put on a scale
17 Mic check #1
20 Coverage co.
21 Gets across?
22 Like a sad sack
23 Long, long time
24 Within: Prefix
26 Mic check #2
31 Like hawks and auks
32 Words to an "old chap"
33 Genetic letters
36 Fix up
37 One of the Jacksons
39 Utah national park
40 A no. that's good when under 3.00
41 Laundromat loss, maybe
42 A beatnik may beat it
43 Mic check #3
47 Minister to
48 Carry on
49 Burger King or The Gap
52 Call after a toss
54 Toward the rear
57 Mic check #4
60 ___ Sea, east of the Ustyurt Plateau
61 Italian wine town
62 Latish bedtime
63 Puts on
64 40-Across, e.g.
65 Campus buys

DOWN

1 "How ___?"
2 Impostor
3 Prefix with second
4 Bull's urging
5 Draw near
6 Move, as a picture
7 Shangri-la
8 Sort of
9 Patriotic org.
10 Heretofore
11 Diminish
12 Straddling
13 Eye of ___ (witches' brew need)
18 Straddling
19 Thurber's fantasizer
23 Slightly
25 Straight, at the bar
26 Broken, in a way
27 Constantly
28 1967 war locale
29 Sounds from pens
30 Certain gasket
34 Scrapped, at NASA
35 Before long
37 Sportscaster Madden
38 Conclusive trial
39 Type of court defense
41 Court reporter
42 One in charge
44 Photos
45 Like dusk
46 Something seen with the Virgin Mary
49 Election hanger-on?
50 Sub
51 Actor Rickman
53 Prov. bordering Mont.
54 Michael J. Fox's role on "Family Ties"
55 Cyclist's problem
56 Some gobblers
58 Suffers from
59 Vane dir.

by Brendan Emmett Quigley

ACROSS

1 Gobbled
6 "___ Lisa"
10 Press down
14 Deep performer
15 Parts of Japanese bridal costumes
16 S-shaped curve
17 Reunion group
18 It comes out of a trunk
19 Monthly expense
20 Was evasive
23 Spleen
24 Good news for an angel
25 Emulated Ethel Merman
33 Old Chevys
34 "Time's a-wastin'!"
35 Salon application
36 Outstanding
37 Oozes
39 Robin Cook thriller
40 Material for a whitesmith
41 Arizona river
42 Having more karats
43 Stake
47 Wedded
48 Colorado native
49 Worse than slapped
58 Toll unit, sometimes
59 "Got it"
60 Wedge drivers
61 Sinn ___
62 Plumlike fruit
63 Plumbing fitting
64 Grandson of Adam
65 Setters
66 Snappish

DOWN

1 Primer material
2 Make a deal with the feds, say
3 Actor Morales
4 "Back in the ___"
5 Document attachments
6 Worked by hand
7 Final notice
8 "The Secret of ___" (1982 animated film)
9 Danger in old homes
10 Some sculptures
11 Seemingly forever
12 Remote control button
13 Fountain of music
21 "A little ___ the mightiest Julius fell": Shak.
22 Bit of Kurdistan
25 ___ State (Arkansas nickname)
26 Roulette bets
27 Shaver
28 Main
29 Person in a mask
30 They're released
31 Shea player, for short
32 A mask, for a 29-Down
33 Punishment for some kids
37 Beans or rice
38 "Bingo, ___ Yale" (fight song)
39 Nod, maybe
41 Characteristic carrier
42 Bump
44 Some coins
45 Pupils
46 Biblical verb ending
49 Dependable
50 Alternatives to mules
51 Advertiser's award
52 Beach site
53 Gaudy sign
54 "Six Feet Under" son
55 "This Love of ___" (1945 film)
56 Thin strip
57 Glimpse

by Nancy Kavanaugh

ACROSS
1 Many a Standardbred
8 Aid in raising cane?
15 San Remo setting
16 One who's trying
17 Member of NATO
18 Hard at it
19 Like some checks: Abbr.
20 Rodgers and Hammerstein musical setting
22 Inner: Prefix
23 ___-El (Superman's birth name)
24 It may interfere with delivery
27 10 marks, once
29 Tank top
30 "Just because"
32 City where Mark Twain is buried
36 Foundation, often
37 People known to have germs?
38 Noted Hollywood exec
39 Refuse to change
40 Imposts
42 In headlinese, say
43 Minor expenses
47 Spanish pronoun
48 Baseball's Drabek
49 Man who's taken vows
50 Cottontail's tail
51 RCA rival
54 Catch
56 Target of a flick
57 Moped
58 They send up jets
59 Things fault-finders study

DOWN
1 It may require joint checking
2 Popular side
3 Rulers' rulers
4 The earth is on one
5 Kind of service
6 Novelist Jünger
7 Fireplace alternative
8 Austrian physician whose work laid the foundation for hypnosis
9 Digital communication?: Abbr.
10 11-member grp.
11 Be on easy street
12 Checking out
13 Kappa's position
14 Cereal killer
21 Pull ___ on
24 Jelly plant
25 "Band of Gold" singer Payne
26 Lets up
28 Broadway sights
31 Assist
33 Curse
34 No longer worried
35 Hill predators
37 Statement made with a tsk, tsk
39 ___ record
41 Cloisonné clusters
43 Label
44 Wild West justice
45 Hardly hard
46 Cavalry soldier
50 Judgment passer, perhaps
52 Boiling blood
53 Tender place?
55 "___ wise guy, eh?"

by Sherry O. Blackard

6

ACROSS

1 Better Business Bureau concerns
6 Hefty competition
10 What someone who is out might be in
14 Put through the mill?
15 Legal cover-up?
16 Robert Burns title starter
17 1986 rock autobiography
18 Member of a small family
20 "Six Degrees of Separation" family name
22 Suitor's presentation
23 Where to spend birr
24 John of Parliament
25 It's projected
30 Browsers' place
32 Sturdy building material
33 Pique experience?
34 Make a stink?
35 Density symbol, in physics
37 It may follow an etym.
39 Ottoman officer
40 Utter
42 Special ability
44 Burrowing animal
46 Mysterious letter writer, maybe
49 Lyricist Dubin and others
50 Come this close
53 Take, as a life
56 Humored
57 Curved wall used as a stage background
59 Actress Georgia ___ of "The Mary Tyler Moore Show"

60 "Flower Petal Gown" sculptor
61 Not easily angered
62 Surgical tube
63 Ones that may get ticked?
64 Gathering suffix
65 "Me, too"

DOWN

1 Sudden increase
2 Get the job done
3 Putting two and two together, say
4 Bring up
5 Pirate
6 "Beethoven" star, 1992
7 Time of many a fairy tale
8 Good enough to 2-Down

9 "The Partridge Family" actress
10 Collusion
11 Votes overseas
12 M.'s counterpart
13 Contributes
19 Swamp thing
21 Bad words
24 "Me, too"
26 See 51-Down
27 Not mincing words?
28 European capital
29 Virginie, e.g.
30 Dos into seis
31 "If a ___ is happy, it cannot fit too close": O. Henry
36 Mama bear, in Madrid
38 Keep
41 It can be semi-attached

43 "The Murder Room" novelist
45 Token
47 Kids' TV character voiced by Kevin Clash
48 One of "Them"
51 With 26-Down, it may be used in a pool
52 Longtime Chicago Symphony conductor
53 Sent a duplicate, briefly
54 Invention of Hermes, supposedly
55 ___ gratuit (something done without apparent motive)
56 Give up, slangily
58 Make calls

by Eric Berlin

ACROSS

1 What a surfer rides
5 Do agricultural work
9 Pre-euro German money
14 Violinist Leopold
15 Side squared, for a square
16 When added up
17 Porn classification
19 AM/FM device
20 Rainbow's shape
21 Attractive
23 Nova ___
26 Battle exhortations
27 Followers of the Vatican
29 Dockworker's org.
30 Postponed
31 Driver entitled to free maps, perhaps
37 Sprinted
38 Grp. battling consumer fraud
39 Genetic letters
40 Big shoe request
44 Accumulate
46 Lumberjack's tool
47 Binds, as wounds
49 Sign-making aids
54 Gets the soap off
55 Part of a grandfather clock
56 "Then what . . .?"
57 Handy ___ (good repairmen)
58 English king during the American Revolution
63 Feed, as a fire
64 Jazz's Fitzgerald
65 Horse color
66 Customs
67 Leave in, to a proofreader
68 At the ocean's bottom, as a ship

DOWN

1 Floor application
2 Secondary, as an outlet: Abbr.
3 Annoy
4 Inconsistent
5 Wealthy sort, slangily
6 ___ Ben Canaan of "Exodus"
7 Extend a subscription
8 ___ cum laude
9 Act of God
10 Horrid glances from Charles Grodin?
11 Hub projections
12 Kevin of "A Fish Called Wanda"
13 Wades (through)
18 Stand up
22 Bad, as a prognosis
23 Mold's origin
24 Something not really on Mars
25 Hypothesize
28 Kemo ___ (the Lone Ranger)
32 Pres. Lincoln
33 Help in crime
34 Button material
35 Follow
36 Metal filers
41 Beard named for a Flemish artist
42 Forgives
43 Astronaut Armstrong
44 Imitating
45 Darners
48 Mount where an ark parked
49 Charley horse, e.g.
50 ___-one (long odds)
51 Witch of ___
52 Olympic sleds
53 Refine, as metal
59 Bullring call
60 Debtor's note
61 Writer Fleming
62 It's kept in a pen

by Patrick Merrell

8

ACROSS

1 "___ as I can tell . . ."
6 Hurdles for future attorneys: Abbr.
11 Pudding fruit
14 Florida's Key ___
15 Florida's ___ Center
16 Form 1040 datum: Abbr.
17 Danish theologian (speller's nightmare #1)
19 Swe. neighbor
20 "As I Lay Dying" character
21 Afternoon: Sp.
22 What "nobody can" do, in song
23 Musical for which Liza Minnelli won a 1978 Tony
25 "___ it a shame"
27 German philosopher (speller's nightmare #2)
32 Walloped, old-style
35 Learning style
36 Cpl., for one
37 Astronomical ring
38 Pipe cleaner
40 20's touring cars
41 First daughter in the Carter White House
42 Certain Scandinavian
43 With regrets
44 Swedish statesman (speller's nightmare #3)
48 Locked (up)
49 Printing goofs
52 Romulus or Remus
54 City maps
57 Seldom seen
59 Colonial ___
60 Russian composer (speller's nightmare #4)
62 "Out of sight!"
63 Freak out
64 Navel variety
65 Brit. lawmakers
66 Reliance
67 Ceaselessly

DOWN

1 ___-Seltzer
2 Francis or Patrick, e.g.
3 Sassy
4 Accepts, as terms
5 Seoul soldier
6 Smooth, in music
7 Trade jabs
8 Military sch.
9 Railed against
10 The "S" in E.S.T.: Abbr.
11 Tweaked
12 Fe, to a chemist
13 Politico Hart
18 Design on metal
22 Cloning need
24 One-spot
26 "___-Devil"
28 Fraternity fun
29 Almost forever
30 Earth Day subj.
31 Pinkish
32 Head of old Iran
33 Papa's partner
34 Quadrennial events
38 Impoverished
39 T.L.C. givers
40 Speed reader?
42 Cheer leader?
43 Camera type, briefly
45 Game pieces
46 On-the-go group
47 Roughly
50 Spoonful, say
51 Alan of "The In-Laws"
52 Time in office
53 Trendy sandwich
55 Island party
56 Dangerous slitherers
58 Ogled
60 Nonunion workers: Abbr.
61 Pooh's pal

by Matt Skoczen

ACROSS

1 High-testing group
6 Drill locale: Abbr.
10 Frisbee, e.g.
14 Huffs and puffs
15 High-priced ticket request
16 ___ family, including bassoons and English horns
17 Very inclined
18 Director Kazan
19 Claimant's claim
20 Flirt's Valentine's gift?
23 Cry after a thoughtful silence
26 ___ the day
27 Enter cautiously
28 One illegally using a handicapped space?
32 Times Sq., e.g., in N.Y.C.
33 Beach Boy Wilson
34 Prospecting bonanzas
36 A dispiritingly large amount of e-mail
37 Extended families
39 ___ West of "Batman"
43 Pale with fright
45 Sticker figure
46 Massage locale
49 www.eyeglasses.com?
52 Crafty
54 Madeira Mrs.
55 "Get the picture?"
56 1960 Terry-Thomas movie (and title of this puzzle)

60 Embroidered ltr., often
61 "Whip It" rock group
62 Grayish
66 Stridex target
67 Sign
68 Wax removers
69 Clutter
70 Rumpelstiltskin's output
71 Flower part

DOWN

1 Mil. go-getters?
2 Proceed after grace
3 Wichita-to-Omaha dir.
4 Potpourri
5 Headache helper
6 Pub container
7 Cherry ___
8 Not fer
9 Maze features
10 Dim bulbs, so to speak
11 Graceful birds
12 "Amen!"
13 Small-plane maker
21 Sister
22 Croupier's tool
23 Getaway stoppers, briefly
24 Heavenly strings
25 "Dite alla giovine," e.g.
29 ___ sutra
30 Steak cut
31 Saturn model
35 Hindu wrap
37 Messy dish to eat
38 Spy novelist Deighton
40 Lodgings, informally
41 Tummy trouble
42 Parcel (out)
44 Neglected neighborhood
45 Things to mind
46 Dr. Seuss character
47 Frolic
48 Diet doctor
50 Donny or Marie
51 "Rin Tin Tin" TV night: Abbr.
53 Honors grandly
57 Verne captain
58 First name in daredevils
59 Toy with a tail
63 Chill
64 Univ. figure
65 Designer monogram

by Lee Glickstein and Nancy Salomon

ACROSS

1. "You wish!"
5. Win every game
10. The gamut
14. A Turner
15. Babe Ruth's ___ was retired
16. Actress Anderson
17. Earthy deposit
18. Arabian Sea sight
19. Capone's nemeses
20. Start of a quip
22. Like most sonnets
24. Thousand ___, Calif.
25. Home of Pottawattamie County
26. Quip, part 2
32. William ___, attorney general under Bush the elder
33. Plug away
34. Swell place?
35. Wild revelry
36. "Bye Bye Bye" band
38. Bank holding
39. "The Matrix" role
40. He broke with Stalin in 1948
41. 20 providers
42. Quip, part 3
47. Gross
48. When Hamlet dies
49. Smallest of the U.S. Virgin Islands
52. End of the quip
56. Faucet brand
57. Samuel Gompers's org., informally
59. Presidential ___
60. Tangelo trademark
61. Madame Tussaud
62. All alternative
63. Rash treatment
64. Switches around
65. Flag feature

DOWN

1. Michigan's ___ College
2. Auto import
3. Crucifix inscription
4. Hawking
5. See 40-Down
6. During the time that
7. Peer of Agatha
8. Letters on some pumps
9. Like a planetary orbit
10. "The Long Goodbye" director, 1973
11. Dead center?
12. R.E.M.'s "The ___ Love"
13. Much of a penny
21. China's Sun ___-sen
23. Gone wrong?
25. Barge ___
26. Seven-time A.L. batting champ
27. Vacuum tube filler
28. "Look ___!"
29. Question in Matthew
30. Swarms
31. Without
32. "With or Without You" singer
36. Handle
37. Dog command
38. Some dwellers on the Baltic
40. With 5-Down, some volatile investments
43. Not entirely human
44. Deemed appropriate
45. Lycées, e.g.
46. Old communications giant
49. Skin flicks and such
50. Forum wear
51. Become definite
52. Shapes with holes
53. Hilarious one
54. Novelist O'Brien
55. A couple of bucks, say
58. It's in one year and out the other

by Scot Ober

ACROSS

1 Popular Bravo series, informally
9 Quaint hairstyle
15 Outraged
16 Insight
17 "Servant of the Bones" writer
18 "This I gotta hear"
19 It's flaky
20 Like a certain complex
21 Per ___
24 March sound
25 Weeklong holiday
26 "The Wizard of Oz" co-star
27 Of the bicuspid valve
29 Annual contributions may be made to them
30 One of 52 in Las Vegas
34 First name in horror
35 Dries up
36 Maupassant's "___ Vie"
37 Where a specialist has expertise
39 Develop
40 Develop
41 Develop
42 Way off
44 Like Brahms's Symphony No. 3
45 Workers' incentives
46 Things included in a count
48 Bristol locale: Abbr.
49 Join forces?
50 It may raise the roof
54 Hebrew title of respect for God
55 Rosary bead representation
56 Zapper
57 Serves

DOWN

1 In the capacity of
2 Broadcaster since Jan. 1995
3 Article of Cologne
4 They may be sworn
5 Hole-in-one, e.g.
6 Pine Valley soap siren
7 Place to work out
8 A storm heading: Abbr.
9 Caused to swell up
10 Snake or eel, e.g.
11 Assign an alias
12 Delicate breakfast item
13 Bravura
14 Break
20 Performed better than, in a way
21 Kind of powder
22 R.B.I. recordholder
23 Annual, e.g.
24 Dialectal pronoun
27 Bidding doers
28 Oils and such
30 Baking holder
31 Masters
32 ___ side (askew)
33 Axolotl look-alikes
35 Bug-eyed cartoon character
38 Irish game resembling field hockey
39 Charging
41 They come from Mars
42 "9 to 5" co-star
43 Fusion
45 Title girl in a Left Banke hit
46 Kind of nectar
47 Levi's uncle
48 VCR alternative
50 Monetary unit?
51 The Rams of the Atlantic 10: Abbr.
52 Yes, in São Paulo
53 Martial arts word meaning "trample" in Korean

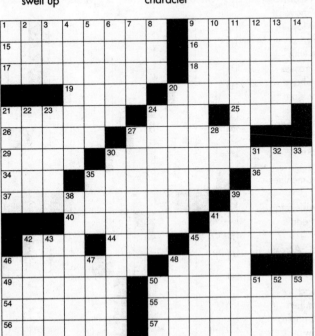

by David Liben-Nowell

12

ACROSS
1 Athletic supporter?
10 Electric meter inventor ___ Thomson
15 Viniculturist's sampling tube
16 Join securely
17 It remains effective until filled or canceled
18 Places to set geraniums
19 Hardly a Yankee fan
20 Flatten, in metalworking
21 Near
22 Brand in the freezer section
24 Prima donna
26 "The Neon Bible" novelist
28 Union foe
29 Shrimp
30 Those with 48-Acrosses
32 It may have reservations
34 Vital
36 Most numbers have two or more
39 Enliven
41 Gym amenities
43 Year in Severus's reign
46 Letterhead?: Abbr.
48 See 30-Across
49 Pros at increasing profits
52 Railroad necessities
53 Series finales
54 Guffaw
56 Setting for St. Paul: Abbr.

57 Country lass
58 Rush hour, in adspeak
60 1,000 millimes
61 Ride
62 Catcher
63 Horoscope data

DOWN
1 Affirmed in court
2 "Put a lid on it!"
3 Not as a group
4 TV dog
5 'Vette option
6 Bit
7 Those who wait
8 Play again
9 About 20% of the earth's land: Abbr.
10 Footnote abbr.
11 Disco-era duds

12 Rather than, with "of"
13 "Stalag 17" star, 1953
14 Still waiting to go out
21 They're changed frequently
23 Option for some long trips
25 "Terrif!"
27 One of die Planeten
31 Antique photos
33 Stink maker
35 Flashy basket
37 Seductive
38 Drummer
40 Male character in French pantomime
42 Some stanzas
43 Ochlophobist's dread

44 Finished
45 "The Third Man" setting
47 Three-person team
50 Three-time World Cup skiing champion
51 Hero, at times
55 Play directors
58 Infielders' stat.
59 Honey eater of New Zealand

by Bob Peoples

ACROSS

1 Food lover's sense
6 Home for alligators
11 "Open ___ 9" (shop sign)
14 Pays to play poker
15 Talk show group
16 Early afternoon hour
17 "Pronto!"
19 Tribe related to the Hopi
20 Historic times
21 Use a hose on, as a garden
23 Rev. William who originated the phrase "a blushing crow"
27 "What so ___ we hailed . . ."
29 Singer Don of the Eagles
30 Opt for
31 Parking lot posting
32 Dahl who wrote "Charlie and the Chocolate Factory"
33 Subject of "worship"
36 Sound in a cave
37 Pocketbook
38 Ditty
39 Itsy-bitsy
40 Free-for-all
41 "I do" sayer
42 "Tom ___" (#1 Kingston Trio hit)
44 Smashed and grabbed
45 Adds up (to)
47 "___ keepers . . ."
48 Boxing matches
49 Skin soother

50 Sphere
51 "Pronto!"
58 Gibson who was People magazine's first Sexiest Man Alive
59 Hair-raising
60 Dickens's ___ Heep
61 "Later!"
62 Coral ridges
63 Shindig

DOWN

1 Bar bill
2 At ___ rate
3 Mudhole
4 Golf ball support
5 Ancient Jewish sect
6 Javelin
7 The "W" in V.F.W.
8 Plus

9 "Oh, give ___ home . . ."
10 Layered building material
11 "Pronto!"
12 Computer chip company
13 Suspicious
18 Card below a four
22 "The Sound of Music" setting: Abbr.
23 Nagging sort
24 Result of a treaty
25 "Pronto!"
26 Skillet lubricant
27 Moon stage
28 Part in a play
30 Actor Feldman
32 Contest specifications
34 Below

35 Requires
37 Hit with snowballs, say
38 Walked on
40 Loch Ness dweller, they say
41 Studies hard
43 Ump's call
44 Animal with a cub
45 Mushroom cloud maker
46 Amsterdam of "The Dick Van Dyke Show"
47 Goes by jet
49 "___ I care!"
52 Part of a giggle
53 Bad temper
54 ___ la la
55 Atmosphere
56 Turner who led a revolt
57 "___ will be done"

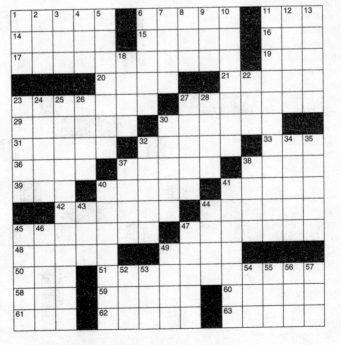

by Gregory E. Paul

14

ACROSS

1 Military bigwigs
6 Pad user
11 Gullible one
14 Consume
15 Luau serving
17 Wine bouquet
18 Consider, as a thought
19 Periodic arrival that causes much angst
21 Big times
22 Hardly a he-man
23 Member of a board of dirs.
24 Flower part
28 ___ Paulo
29 ___-all (score)
30 Really good joke
34 Seat at a wedding
37 What a 52-Across on a group of 19-Acrosses is
40 Whitney and others: Abbr.
41 Aim
42 Roman writer
43 Some Harvard grads: Abbr.
44 Certain Wall Street activities
46 Some are pale
48 La ___
51 Money guarantor, for short
52 Student's dream
57 "Hail, Stanford, Hail!," for one
59 Swashbuckling Flynn
60 Song from "No, No, Nanette"
61 Aptly named English novelist
62 Yearbook sect.
63 Kind of code at some schools
64 "The Sixth ___"

DOWN

1 Symbol on California's flag
2 Like a 52-Across
3 On
4 Clash of heavyweights
5 Spread out
6 Writer's guidelines
7 Turner and Louise
8 Diary bit
9 Penury
10 Sculler
11 Flat replacement
12 TV spy series starring Jennifer Garner
13 What stylophiles collect
16 Wing: Prefix
20 Equipment in kids' toy "telephones"
23 Prefix with legal
24 Dis
25 Perfectly
26 Gardner and others
27 ___ culpa
28 "Frasier" setting
31 Cereal grain
32 Actress Charlotte
33 Dodge City's home: Abbr.
34 Invoice stamp
35 House shader
36 Methods
38 Broadcasts
39 Like
43 Coffee for late at night
45 Go-carts
46 Grace ___ of "Will & Grace"
47 Certain beans
48 Tre + quattro
49 Ships' workers
50 Big dos
51 Saturated substances
52 Henry VIII's sixth
53 Place for a knot
54 Mother's mother, informally
55 Miniature sci-fi vehicles
56 Sheltered, at sea
58 Stylish, in the 60's

by Kevan Choset

ACROSS

1 "Poppycock!"
5 Iraqi port
10 Thompson of "Family"
14 Big name in oil
15 In-box contents
16 Wife, in legalese
17 Line to Penn Station
18 Sweater for the cold-blooded?
20 Cold-blooded idler?
22 TV extraterrestrial
23 Corrida cries
24 1983 Keaton title role
28 Microwave setting
30 Property receiver, in law
32 Latin 101 verb
33 Soaps, to soap operas, once
34 Cold-blooded dice roll?
38 Pit crew member
41 Salinger lass
45 Testified
46 English port
49 Tapir feature
50 Long, long time
51 Fictitious Richard
52 Cold-blooded children's play activity?
56 Cold-blooded fungi?
59 Samoan capital
60 Last of the Stuarts
61 Reason for a raise
62 Shape with a hammer
63 Stuff
64 Straws in the wind
65 Once, once

DOWN

1 Chaucerian verse form
2 1969 Mets victims
3 Napes
4 Gunpowder holder
5 Narcotic-yielding palms
6 Talisman
7 Calcutta wraps
8 Classic hotel name
9 __ breve
10 Summer attire
11 Send packing
12 One of a Disney septet
13 Pairs holder?
19 Regal fur
21 Sticky stuff
25 Phone trigram
26 Key contraction?
27 __ amis
29 Assume anew, as burdens
30 Barbary beast
31 Powell co-star in 1930's films
33 Jiffy
35 1598 edict city
36 "Wheel of Fortune" buy
37 A little butter?
38 Hosp. staffers
39 Velvet finish?
40 Navy noncom
42 Bass variety
43 Professors World Peace Academy group, informally
44 White-tie, say
46 Once-divided place
47 Homing pigeons' homes
48 Having one sharp
50 Prior to, in dialect
53 Air: Prefix
54 Feature of many a sympathy card
55 Get an eyeful
56 Put out
57 No longer divided
58 Collection suffix

by A. J. Santora

16

ACROSS

1. ___ Morris, signature on the Declaration of Independence
5. Untanned
9. Enthusiastic about
14. Home of the Rainbow Bridge National Monument
15. City near Stillwater
16. Second-largest lake in North America
17. Carry
18. 1984 Peace Nobelist
19. What to say to a kahuna
20. Ballpark fare
23. Ready
24. Engine need
25. Casa ___ (Italian restaurant name)
28. Born
29. Sources of soft feathers
32. Admission seeker, maybe: Abbr.
33. Secret grp. since 1947
34. Hook, line or sinker
35. "Stop!"
36. Come down hard
40. Parts of a V formation
42. Norway's patron saint
43. Currency shop abbr.
46. Hike
47. Infer
49. Pal of Piglet
50. Cask material
51. Formerly "cursed" team, informally
52. Summer worker
54. It might pick up a few pointers
57. Aviary sound
60. Came down
61. Duel tool
62. Bursting stars
63. Superboy's girlfriend
64. Give it ___
65. "___ is human . . ."
66. RR employee
67. Kids' closetful

DOWN

1. Soprano Swenson
2. Actors Peter and Annette
3. Kellogg's home
4. Things can go to them
5. Start of an initiative
6. "Sometimes you feel like ___ . . ."
7. Printing technique: Abbr.
8. Professor
9. "Adventures in moving" sloganeer, once
10. ___-free
11. One way to swing
12. Cry at fireworks
13. Part of a cell nucleus
21. Wimp
22. Bro's sibling
25. Meet
26. Return destination?: Abbr.
27. Decoration
30. Old gold coin
31. Belgian painter James
32. Lassie, for one
35. Coming
37. Put to
38. 2001 biopic
39. International Harvester vehicle maker
40. "Little" car of song
41. Constitutional proposal first introduced in Cong. in 1923
44. Harry Potter's forte
45. Democratic symbols
47. Sawbones
48. Yoga instruction
51. Disperse
53. Milk-Bone biscuit, e.g.
54. Certain bookmark
55. Dash
56. Encircle
57. Bang maker
58. Ply with wine and flowers, say
59. Christmas ___

by Roy Leban

ACROSS

1 Not blocked
5 Knocked completely off one's feet
15 What a card reader may do?
16 For love or money
17 Dejection interjection
18 It's used to make carbon black
19 Pool opening
21 Like some hands
22 It's nice when prize winnings come with lots of these
23 Meddle managers?
24 Town near Perugia
27 Blazed
28 Wars of the Roses battle site
31 Coupe complement
34 Permanently undecided
35 Gallery item
36 1969 target
37 Head up North?
38 Noted 2003 Eton graduate
42 Pan, e.g.
43 Peak
44 Application after a break
47 Reason to put on a collar
49 Sash accompanier, maybe
50 War game
54 Line of sight?
56 Inter __
57 Events for potential bidders
58 Artery
59 Using big words?
60 Lively

DOWN

1 Moore verse opener
2 Counseling, e.g.
3 Bring up
4 Expanding
5 Punch with punch
6 Aviator __ Balbo
7 "Princess Caraboo" star, 1994
8 Currency unit in Harry Potter tales
9 Strathclyde port
10 Some earth movers
11 Francis of old TV
12 Probe
13 Florida's __ National Forest
14 Exploits
20 Make a home
23 Thither
24 Contemporary of Emerson
25 Bellow in a library
26 Send down
27 Barber's supply
29 Cut off the back
30 Crib
31 Reason to press a suit, perhaps
32 Sported
33 Black
36 Nougat-filled treats
38 Dash
39 Progress preventer
40 Superlatively smooth
41 Pressure
42 Activity on a range
44 Milker's aid
45 Browning title character
46 "Ciao!"
47 Persian
48 Rouse
50 Fear, to François
51 Cockeyed
52 Iago, e.g.
53 Disney dog
55 Letter lineup

by Craig Kasper

18

ACROSS

1 National service
9 Buggy
15 How some entrees are served
16 Cut aid
17 "Don't sweat it"
18 Palace figures
19 Mass apparel
20 Part of a column
22 Animal that Poseidon turned Theophane into, in myth
23 Year in Nero's reign
24 Land
25 Unrest
26 Lamp sites
28 All over
29 Biblical verb
30 Bash
32 Neutral shades
34 Fork-tailed bird
35 Ending of some plant names
36 Classic convertible name
39 Murphy's portrayer
42 Dredge (up)
43 They're all for it
45 A month abroad
47 Somalian-born supermodel
48 Swinger
50 "Cupid is a knavish ___": "A Midsummer Night's Dream"
51 Part of a footnote abbr.
52 Jewish village
53 Zaire's Mobutu ___ Seko
54 One to watch in a pinch?
56 Matter of course
58 Attach securely
59 Drinkers, at times
60 Magnetic induction units
61 Cruising

DOWN

1 Presidential first name
2 Unfolds
3 Wimp
4 Speaker of note
5 Cape Tres Puntas locale: Abbr.
6 ". . . but no ___"
7 Environmentalist's concern
8 Grooves on a coin's edge
9 Snack named for a Massachusetts town
10 Like Hawaiian shirts
11 Boise's county
12 Relative of a bug
13 Back to back
14 Takes off wrongly
21 Period of darkening
24 "Rich Man, Poor Man" actor, 1976
25 Recluse
27 Term of affection
31 Surprise court actions
33 Warwickshire forest
35 Accusatory question
36 Fair
37 "It's Too Late Now" autobiographer
38 Camel performers
39 Totals
40 Former name of Sulawesi
41 Sign of a slip
44 Mus. slow-up
46 Texas city named by Russian immigrants
49 ___ once
52 Old gathering place
53 1960's–70's Japanese leader
55 NATO member since 1999: Abbr.
57 D-Day vessel: Abbr.

by Rich Norris

ACROSS

1 Big blowout
5 Vehicles with meters
9 Like some committees
14 Charles Lamb's nom de plume
15 Cookie with creme inside
16 Takes a card from the pile
17 Where to order egg salad
18 Flintstone fellow
19 Designer Karan
20 Practically gives away
23 Whole lot
24 Restless
27 Bandleader Shaw
29 Big galoots
31 "Vive le ___!"
32 Faint from rapture
33 Waterless
34 Mulligatawny, for one
35 Starts telling a different story
38 Theme park attraction
39 Bringing up the rear
40 Magician's rods
41 Gallery display
42 One who's suckered
43 Voting districts
44 Pushed snow aside
46 Saucy
47 Prepares to be punished
53 Desperately want
55 Homeboy's turf
56 Hurry up
57 Macho guys
58 English princess
59 River in an Agatha Christie title
60 Apply, as pressure
61 Not the original color
62 Meal in a pot

DOWN

1 People retire to these spots
2 Toward the sheltered side
3 Window feature
4 Dangerous bit of precipitation
5 Morning eyeopener
6 Turn signal
7 Brewski
8 Word after baking or club
9 Extras
10 Speak in a monotone
11 Loiter
12 Part of B.Y.O.B.
13 Jefferson Davis org.
21 David's weapon, in the Bible
22 Soft leather
25 Pings and dings
26 "Holy mackerel!"
27 Spinning
28 Celebrity's upward path
29 Cropped up
30 Pub offering
32 Throw out
33 "On the double!"
34 Bravura performances
36 Escape the detection of
37 Bunch of bees
42 Not half bad
43 Pulled dandelions, say
45 Be indecisive
46 Give a buzz
48 Certain herring
49 Chichi
50 Clubs or hearts
51 Capri, for one
52 Enjoy some gum
53 Friend of Fidel
54 Mystery author Stout

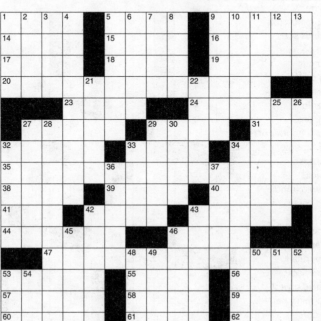

by Nancy Salomon and Kendall Twigg

ACROSS

1 "60 Minutes" airer
4 Gator relative
8 Nyasaland, now
14 Stephen of "The Crying Game"
15 Quad building
16 Readied for print
17 Post-O.R. stop
18 Meat marking
19 Brings disgrace to
20 Knowing no more than before
23 Part of a Vandyke
24 Mangy mutt
25 Stitch up
28 Lanchester of film
29 Words after a rude encounter, maybe
33 "___ extra cost!"
34 Devious sorts
35 One pointing, as a gun
39 Feel awful
41 Secret meeting
42 Mazola competitor
44 Gets a gander of
46 F.B.I.'s prime quarries
48 Twofold
52 Dr. who handles otitis cases: Abbr.
53 Neolithic ___
54 Where Idi Amin ruled
56 Buffet deal
59 Positive aspect
62 Swarming pest
63 Bio stat
64 Gawks
65 Low-cal
66 D.C. V.I.P.
67 Lecherous goat-men
68 Divorcés
69 Sink trap's shape

DOWN

1 Shrink in fear
2 Act nonchalant
3 Steamy spots
4 Water park slide
5 Most reckless
6 Shoppe sign word
7 Lobster portion
8 Snafus
9 Followers
10 Pants-on-fire guy
11 20's dispenser, for short
12 Teeny
13 Driver's lic. and others
21 Airport info: Abbr.
22 Convenience store bagful
25 Neuter
26 Part of B.P.O.E.
27 All-star game team, maybe
30 ___ roll (winning)
31 Like tasty cake
32 Anthem contraction
33 Metal joiner
35 Very top
36 Mineral in spinach
37 Atomizer's release
38 N.Y. winter setting
40 General in gray
43 Like a rowboat that's adrift
45 Teach
47 Dissenting vote
48 Vice president Quayle
49 Apprehension
50 Almanac sayings
51 Nears midnight
55 Billionaire Bill
56 Open-roofed
57 Leer at
58 Operating system on many Internet servers
59 ___ Constitution
60 Sch. group
61 Warmed the bench

by Nancy Kavanaugh

ACROSS

1 When doubled, a seafood entree
5 Is visibly frightened
10 Off one's trolley
14 "Yeah, right!"
15 Work ___
16 Pop's Brickell
17 Gigantic instrument?
19 "Take ___!" (track coach's order)
20 Holed up
21 First name in horror
22 Actress Sorvino
23 Instrument made in the lab?
27 Straits of ___
28 Tee follower?
29 Crew need
30 Set alight
33 Quattros, e.g.
37 Greet the day
39 Take your pick?
41 Federico of the Clinton cabinet
42 Touch up
44 Up
46 Early fifth-century year
47 Ridge of Homeland Security
49 Like some burgers
51 Instrument found at the Super Bowl?
56 Donald, to Dewey
57 Opposite of paleo-
58 Order of corn
59 "I'll be ___ of a gun!"
60 Missing instrument?
65 Ste. Jeanne ___
66 King of Thebes slain by Theseus
67 Inner: Prefix
68 January 1 song word
69 Surfer wannabe
70 Mail: Abbr.

DOWN

1 Shelley queen
2 "___ recall . . ."
3 Arrogant one's place
4 More uncertain
5 Chips' place
6 1955 merger grp.
7 Eric Clapton hit with a never-ending chorus
8 Flynn of "Captain Blood"
9 Dumpster emanation
10 Request to the Enterprise
11 Seat-of-the-pants performance
12 Papal wear
13 Calyx part
18 ___ one
23 Miner's filing
24 Binding exchanges
25 Magna ___
26 Roll-call call
27 "Watch out!"
31 P.C. part
32 When repeated, a cry of approval
34 U.S. citizen-to-be
35 The Dow, e.g.
36 Port ___ (Suez Canal city)
38 Door
40 1991 Grammy winner Cohn
43 Point
45 Keepsake
48 Good guy
50 Sanford of "The Jeffersons"
51 Thigh muscles
52 Take back
53 Squirrel's find
54 Old, but new again
55 Like unpopular umps
61 Mauna ___
62 Omega
63 Orch. section
64 Brillo rival

by Eric and Janinne Berlin

ACROSS

1 Artist Chagall
5 Put on hold
11 Internet letters, and a hint to this puzzle's theme
14 It's sold in bars
15 Two-legged salamander
16 Source of heat
17 Nirvana, essentially?
19 Potassium hydroxide
20 Right and left
21 Anonymous
23 Dealership that sells old Troopers?
27 Handsome prints?
29 Easy win
30 It ends in Oct.
31 Question from Miss Piggy
32 Tissue: Suffix
34 Handwriting on the wall
38 Hollywood favorite
40 Socialite Brooke
42 Memorization technique
43 Withhold from
44 Vaughan of jazz
46 "On the double!"
47 ___ draft
50 "Au revoir!"
51 Small colonist
52 Long forks, for example?
57 1967 Oscar winner Parsons
58 Toys sometimes stuck in trees
61 Shoe part
62 Certain Hawaiian instrument?
66 2002 British Open champion

67 Freud's home
68 Number for one
69 Shooting site
70 Went for a bite
71 Dermatologist's concern

DOWN

1 Mineral hardness scale inventor
2 Others, in Latin
3 Certain delivery
4 They may be cracked
5 Western Athletic Conf. school
6 Home for a hermit
7 Shogun's capital
8 Constellation known as the Hare
9 Like marble

10 Herd in Africa
11 Buck Rogers's lady friend
12 More twisted
13 Groundskeeper's bane
18 Assume
22 One with a part
24 Defender of Manet's work
25 Minutemen of coll. sports
26 Like Albany and Chicago
27 In the thick of
28 Went on
33 Capone rival known as Bugs
35 Quiet home, usually
36 Royal educator
37 Witches' brew necessity

39 Old "Hollywood Squares" regular
41 "Doggone it!"
45 Three-line work
48 "One great face deserves another" sloganeer, once
49 Café specification
52 Swanky dos
53 "___ Mio"
54 Explosive trial
55 Snicker
56 Purple shade
59 George and George W., e.g.
60 Musical chairs goal
63 Game with a 108-card deck
64 Burma's first P.M.
65 Kit ___

by Greg Staples

ACROSS

1 Home of America's first automatic traffic light, ca. 1920
16 Declaration of independence
17 Store something away, in a way
18 Raised rumblers
19 "One Mic" rapper
20 Western N.C.A.A. powerhouse
21 Workout unit
22 Southpaw Shawn
24 N.S. clock setting
27 ___ Drake, longtime illustrator of "Blondie"
30 Actor Corey ___
34 Mrs. Reed's creator
39 "That's my final offer"
40 It's surprising when played
41 Record problem
42 Shift very carefully
43 Fronted
44 Personal assts. keep track of them
48 A question of self-examination
51 Follower of Christ?
52 Cartoon hit
55 Sun Devils' sch.
58 Superpowers often have them
62 1959 pop hit that asked "Why?"
63 Infatuation situation

DOWN

1 Element of change
2 Series follower: Abbr.
3 "Bad!" sounds
4 Explorer of the Canadian Arctic
5 P. D. James's "Death ___ Expert Witness"
6 "Garfield" waitress
7 Tight ends?
8 What androphobes fear
9 Metrical stress
10 Vacation locale, with "the"
11 Mozart's portrayer in "Amadeus"
12 Vacation spot
13 Classic cars that were the first to have Ram Air engines
14 Giotto's work
15 Reply put in by Putin?
22 Some like them hot
23 Be rude in line
24 Be temporarily
25 Radio___
26 Original "Star Trek" actor
27 Bad thing to have showing
28 Threatener of Miss Gulch
29 Buckets
31 Slippery as ___
32 Stick-to-___
33 Dealt
35 Commits to another hitch
36 The lady in "The Lady From Shanghai"
37 Former first lady's first name
38 Breathing abnormality
45 Firing places
46 Zhou ___
47 Think fit
48 Politico Hutchinson and others
49 Slugger Williams
50 Virginia willow
52 Universal Postal Union headquarters
53 Japon's place
54 Range: Abbr.
55 "That's not ___!" (parent's admonishment)
56 Golf's Ballesteros
57 Handles
59 Suffix with cannon
60 ___ Fabi of auto racing
61 It contains about 6% alcohol by volume

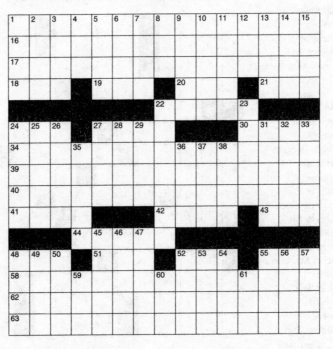

by David Levinson Wilk

24

ACROSS

1 Polo alternative
5 Food item whose name means "slice"
9 The "C" of C. S. Lewis
14 Composition of some ladders
15 Gray ode subject
16 Soda pop purchase
17 Abbr. that may precede a colon
18 Fast talker
20 Like some architectural designs
22 Checks
23 Leading the queue
24 Honolulu's ___ Tower
26 Pulls the plug on
28 Liberal
32 Executive attachment
33 Quaint taletellers
34 ___ mater
35 Divvy up
37 Old faces in workplaces, perhaps
39 Where to go in Gloucester
40 Schubert's "___ sentimentale"
42 In a safe place
43 Lamp locale
45 Pick-me-up
46 Time's partner
47 End of Missouri's motto
48 "The View" co-host
50 Lonely
54 Mom or dad
56 ___ jure (legal phrase)

57 Sipowicz player on "N.Y.P.D. Blue"
58 "What ___?"
59 Commend, as for outstanding service
60 Rosalind's cousin in "As You Like It"
61 Terrarium youngsters
62 Are, in Arles

DOWN

1 Gasconade
2 Learning may be done by it
3 Like a troublemaker
4 Not so tough
5 Spreads
6 It has its notions
7 Fantasia's cousin

8 Dove's helper, in an Aesop tale
9 Person likely to have a big closet
10 Unlike a plane
11 Point
12 Flashed signs
13 Need to be set straight
19 Legendary Irish princess
21 Really big show
25 "Mad Love" star, 1935
26 Red ___
27 Red ___
29 Laetrile source
30 Flower girl, sometimes
31 Stunner
33 Ruby's defender
36 Armor coverer
38 Sooner than soon

41 Dispatch
44 Falafel sauce
45 Plagues
48 Empty
49 Notably secure carrier
51 Put out
52 Town in the Euganean Hills
53 Pulls off
54 One overseen by a sgt.
55 Name associated with anonymity

by Dana Motley

ACROSS

1 Musical genre pioneered by Bill Haley and His Comets
5 Cove
10 Partner of ready and willing
14 Unattractive tropical fruit
15 Voting site
16 Hit with the fist
17 Sunbather's award?
19 Sandwich fish
20 Still
21 Before, in poetry
22 Interpret without hearing
24 1051 on monuments
25 Edward who wrote "The Owl and the Pussycat"
26 Temples in the Far East
30 Assassinating
33 Oldtime actress Massey
34 Join, in woodworking
36 La Paz is its cap.
37 President after Tyler
38 Sun-bleached
39 "__ Ben Adhem," Leigh Hunt poem
40 Finish
41 Duelist Burr
42 Was bright, as the sun
43 Mark for misconduct
45 Gas ratings
47 Kuwaiti leader
48 Sun or planet
49 Depot baggage handlers
52 Actress Joanne
53 Next-to-last Greek letter
56 Wings: Lat.
57 Romantics' awards?
60 1/500 of the Indianapolis 500
61 Have a mad crush on
62 Colorful gem
63 [No bid]
64 Changed direction, as a ship
65 Actor Billy of "Titanic"

DOWN

1 Slippers' color in "The Wizard of Oz"
2 Shrek, for one
3 Blood problem
4 One of the same bloodline
5 Portugal and Spain together
6 Snout
7 Auction unit
8 List-ending abbr.
9 Tickled pink
10 Off course
11 Sad person's award?
12 Moon goddess
13 Old-time exclamation
18 Mrs. F. Scott Fitzgerald
23 Nectar source
24 Neurotic TV detective played by Tony Shalhoub
26 Spoke (up)
27 On one's own
28 Big recording artists' awards?
29 Brainy
30 Dictation taker
31 Nary a soul
32 Affixes (to)
35 Wedding 58-Down
38 Good sportsmanship
39 "Moby-Dick" captain
41 Song for a diva
42 Olympic gymnast Kerri
44 Roasts' hosts
46 __ beef
49 Entrance to an expressway
50 Director Kazan
51 Scotch's partner
52 Dreadful
53 Insect stage
54 Go across
55 __ of Man
58 See 35-Down
59 Family relation, for short

by Bernice Gordon

ACROSS
1 "If it ___ broke . . ."
5 "Guilty," e.g.
9 Clio winner
14 Most stuck-up
16 Poker ploy
17 "M.T.A." singers, 1959
19 Makes merry
20 Chart shape
21 "Bearded" flower
22 Mall binge
25 Murals and such
28 Dover's state: Abbr.
29 Rang out
31 Like gastric juice
32 40 winks
33 Group values
34 Paul Scott chronicles set in India
37 Weather map area
38 Have more troops than
39 Right on the map
40 Response to someone pointing
41 Actress Peeples
44 Take a gander at
45 Make ___ of (botch)
46 U.S.M.C. V.I.P.'s
47 German article
48 Is fearful of
50 Schubert chamber work
56 Fritter away
57 Unusual sort
58 Place for a kiss
59 Hatchling's home
60 Wagnerian earth goddess

DOWN
1 ___ Lindgren, Pippi Longstocking's creator
2 Naturally belong
3 It may be seen, heard or spoken, in a saying
4 Quick puffs
5 A.T.M. necessities
6 Trouser part
7 Pothook shape
8 J.D. holder: Abbr.
9 Golfer Palmer, to pals
10 See socially
11 Former Russian orbiter
12 "___ was saying . . ."
13 Prefix with natal
15 Up to, for short
18 Newspaper page
22 Home of the N.H.L.'s Sharks
23 Awards to be hung
24 Positions of esteem
25 Need liniment
26 Knee-slapper
27 Six-pointers, in brief
29 Hair-splitter?
30 LAX abbr.
31 Envelope abbr.
32 Gumball cost, once
33 The "E" in Q.E.D.
34 Cafeteria carrier
35 Vacuum feature
36 Buddy in Bordeaux
37 Lab charge
40 Mae West's "___ Angel"
41 Less cluttered
42 "You're so right!"
43 Courtroom fig.
45 Broadcaster
46 Sci-fi, for one
47 James of blues
48 The Everly Brothers, e.g.
49 Josh
50 Onetime Pan Am rival
51 Linden of "Barney Miller"
52 Body shop fig.
53 Java container
54 ___ kwon do
55 Football game divs.

by Len Elliott

ACROSS

1 White House affair, maybe
5 Beyond's partner
10 Part of Latin 101 conjugation
14 ___ Bator
15 Measure from the elbow to the end of the middle finger
16 Results may do this
17 With 33-, 36- and 40-Across, American born 7/28/1929
19 Press
20 Hip bone
21 Vital
22 Actress Hayek
23 Boating mishap
24 Neighbor of a Vietnamese
26 Period of time
28 Gary's home: Abbr.
31 Periods of time
32 Off
33 See 17-Across
35 Hall of Fame QB Dawson
36 See 17-Across
37 Name that's an alphabet trio
40 See 17-Across
41 Modern medical grps.
42 Composer/writer Ned
44 Cable inits.
45 Ages and ages
46 Most blue
48 ___-mo
49 Right hands
50 New Deal inits.
53 Celebrity photographer Herb
56 Where D.D.E. went to sch.
57 Topper made popular by 17- and 36-Across
59 Retro phone feature
60 Laughing gas, for one
61 "Born Free" lioness
62 Lodges
63 Baseball datum
64 Part of CBS: Abbr.

DOWN

1 Kodak competitor
2 Mideast carrier
3 Reserved
4 Commission's task
5 Top-notch
6 Mail may be sent in this
7 Award for Tony Kushner
8 Like old records
9 Summer on the Seine
10 Wilbur or Orville Wright
11 Florida player
12 Bouquets
13 "Seduced" senator of film
18 Man in black?
22 Cry on a hog farm
25 During
26 "2001" mainframe
27 See red?
28 Structural members
29 Votes in Versailles
30 Kirsten of "Spider-Man"
34 Marble feature
36 Genuflection points
37 Without a hitch
38 Proverbial brickload
39 Seagoing letters
40 Trials
41 DNA structures
42 Granola ingredient
43 One who's "out"
46 Any of the Fahd ruling family
47 ___ 12 and 20
48 Angel's favorite letters
51 Dancer's exercise
52 13-Down player
54 Itar-___ news agency
55 E.R. order
57 Med. test result
58 ___ canto

by Mark Elliot Skolsky

ACROSS

1 Testing centers
5 Connections
8 Large marine herbivore
14 Yellow spread
15 Short flight
16 State admitted during the Civil War
17 Eyesight impairer
19 Ready to be hung up, say
20 "Simon says pretend you're on a trampoline"
22 "Give it ___!"
23 Calamitous
24 Mischief-maker
27 Club ___
28 Seine feeder
29 High-rise member
30 "Simon says imitate a soldier"
34 Slanting
37 Last name in sharpshooting
38 "Simon says act like a bird"
42 Playwright who coined the term "lothario"
43 Patch up
44 Orlando Predators' grp.
47 Pay off the mortgage on
48 Milk source
49 Kind of lily
51 "Give me a round of applause"
55 Curmudgeon's greeting
57 Ballet featuring the evil magician Von Rothbart
58 Respectful
59 Get into a stew?
60 Strong server
61 Said "one club," e.g.
62 Sung syllable
63 Congressional mtg.

DOWN

1 Lumbering problem
2 Enticement
3 Appeared triumphant
4 Stock options?
5 Breakfast chain, for short
6 Like Bedouins
7 Florida colonizers, with "the"
8 Disparaging
9 Architect Saarinen
10 Acknowledge
11 Friday, for one
12 Work with feet
13 Mouthful
18 Studio shout
21 Eins + zwei
25 Stalker deterrent
26 Stalked one
28 Name on a wafer
29 Sorts
30 Have a long face
31 P.D. alert
32 Direction opposite sud
33 Kitchen spray
34 "The Mod Squad" do
35 School zone warning
36 Result of a house cleaning, maybe
39 1947 film noir starring Dennis O'Keefe
40 Fast-food worker's equipment
41 Pacifistic
44 French border region
45 Some breakfast cereals
46 Hens, e.g.
48 Trifled (with)
49 Aaron Brown's employer
50 World book?
52 High-handed remark?
53 Captain's aide
54 Figures
55 Mailing ctr.
56 Alley ___

by Patrick Merrell

ACROSS

1 Much-seen figure on a security cam
10 "Look out below!," e.g.
15 Going
16 Mann who sang "Save Me," 1999
17 Ninnies
18 Quintain rhyme scheme
19 Make a face
20 Pound sound
21 Old-fashioned news announcer
22 Got down
24 "No kidding!"
26 A or B in blood typing, e.g.
29 Kin of hagfish
30 Kick, in a way
31 Usual
33 Nice amount of moola
36 Eur. kingdom
37 Hardly the screaming type
38 Let go
39 Off one's feed
40 Fuel type, informally
41 They have plans, for short
42 Longtime Delaware senator William
43 Place name in 90's TV
45 Kid's taunt
49 Feature of an exit strategy?
50 "The African Queen" co-star, informally
51 Farm male
53 Bang up
56 ___ Corning, fiberglass maker
57 Integrated with
59 Amtrak station west of Grand Forks
60 Drawing room?
61 First name in sewing
62 [See above]

DOWN

1 Goes up and down
2 Sometime soon
3 Zero
4 Beggar's bearing
5 Baseball hero called "Gibraltar in cleats"
6 Wear and tear
7 Not home
8 Transmit
9 Calling a Jaguar XK a jalopy, say
10 Certain battery
11 Fall guys?
12 Kind of address
13 Not stand for oppression
14 Demonstratively sad
23 Stretching quality
25 Flinched, maybe
26 Prefix with syllabic
27 Wassailer's song
28 Pretty good
32 Preschoolers?
33 Attorneys' productions
34 Some people cry when these are said
35 ___-humanité
38 Major export of Albania and South Africa
40 "No legacy is so rich as ___": Shak.
42 Three-toed critters
44 Was beaten by
45 Certain W.M.D.
46 "That hurts!"
47 Broker
48 Nymph in Muslim paradise
52 Paw
54 Energize
55 You can hang your hat on it
58 "Saving Private Ryan" craft: Abbr.

by Manny Nosowsky

ACROSS

1 1971 Bond girl portrayer
11 It's often given a red coat
15 Something that may be twisted apart
16 Deal
17 Fancied
18 Language of the 1983 film title "Koyaanisqatsi"
19 Contracted into folds
20 They may be blowing in the wind
22 Plus-or-minus fig.
23 1998 name in the news
26 Get set to shoot
27 It may put you in a difficult position
29 Modest
31 Thackeray's "The Book of ___"
33 "It's all ___"
34 Dungeons & Dragons co., once
35 Kind of story
38 G.E. co-founder
41 It may fill up your tank
42 Keep from desiccating
46 Jet-setters
49 Ballyshannon's river
50 Corn problem
51 Conical dryers
53 It's hard to get a grip on
54 Over
56 Shirt that leaves the midriff exposed
58 Applied oneself (to)
59 Request to a cabby
62 Capacity
63 Oscar nominee for "A Man and a Woman"
64 Soprano Ameling
65 Untold

DOWN

1 They're usually short . . . or shorts
2 Affixes, in a way
3 "Move on"
4 Senator who succeeded John Stennis
5 "Gladiator" director
6 Some cartridges' contents
7 Famed streaker of 1941
8 Let pass
9 Chart maker
10 Hardly classicists
11 Making a comeback?
12 Punching bag, so to speak
13 Kind of court
14 Expert, slangily
21 One who may marry repeatedly
24 Supercontinent of 200+ million years ago
25 1998 Ice Cube film, with "The"
28 Exerciser's pride
30 Plasma alternative, for short
32 Lift passages
36 Tied, in a way
37 Thou
38 Globe, e.g.
39 Send a jet over?
40 Dim sum selection
43 Correspondence request
44 Added numbers
45 Mobile homes
47 Something to play
48 Forty-niner's fantasy
52 Aid in removal of mines
55 Arch
57 "Buck Rogers" novelist Nowlan
60 Big name in Burmese history
61 Actor in Pink Panther films

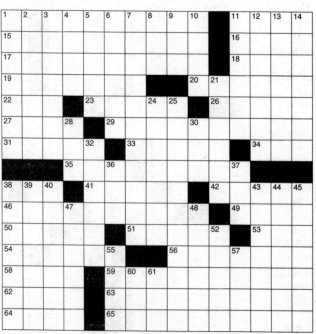

by Byron Walden

ACROSS

1 Mall component
6 Genesis twin
10 Fly like an eagle
14 Hiker's path
15 Goatee's locale
16 Time for eggnog
17 Having no entryways?
19 A.A.A. recommendations: Abbr.
20 Left on a map
21 How some ham sandwiches are made
22 Letter after theta
23 Disney World attraction
25 Opposite of whole, milkwise
27 "French" dog
30 "I'm ready to leave"
32 Down Under bird
33 Britannica, for one: Abbr.
35 "Thanks, Pierre!"
38 Squeal (on)
39 ___ standstill (motionless)
40 City that Fred Astaire was "flying down to" in a 1934 hit
42 "Dear old" family member
43 Jogs
45 Looks sullen
47 Poetic palindrome
48 Tributary
50 Word before Nevada or Leone
52 Hold back
54 Give a benediction to
56 Ball field covering
57 Motionless
59 Campaign funders, for short
63 Buffalo's lake
64 Having no vision?
66 Submarine danger
67 Number between dos and cuatro
68 Weird
69 Habitual tipplers
70 Gumbo vegetable
71 Modify to particular conditions

DOWN

1 Put in the hold
2 "___ Grit" (John Wayne film)
3 Quaker ___
4 Ran amok
5 Santa's little helper
6 Commercial prefix with Lodge
7 In a moment
8 Bright and breezy
9 Still in the out-box, as mail
10 Injection selection
11 Having no commandment?
12 Prince Valiant's wife
13 Plopped down again
18 Museum guide
24 Delighted
26 Gradual absorption method
27 Saucy
28 Bradley or Sharif
29 Having no typeset letters?
31 Stocking shade
34 Where to watch whales in Massachusetts, with "the"
36 Writer John Dickson ___
37 Inkling
41 "The only thing we have to fear is fear ___": F.D.R.
44 Prairie homes
46 It goes around the world
49 Mississippi River explorer
51 Caught sight of
52 Agenda details
53 The first part missing in the author's name ___ Vargas ___
55 The second part missing in the author's name ___ Vargas ___
58 Istanbul resident
60 Taj Mahal locale
61 Intel product
62 Typesetting mark
65 Poseidon's domain

by Holden Baker

32

ACROSS

1 Sir, in India
6 Gounod production
11 Word with toll or roll
14 ___ acid
15 Cartoonist Kelly and others
16 Singer on half the 1984 album "Milk and Honey"
17 Hard-to-please labor protester?
19 Bird's beak
20 ¢¢¢
21 Unc's wife
23 Busta Rhymes rhymes
27 Like some of the Sahara
28 Flies off the handle
29 West Indian native
30 Mar. 17 figure, from 58-Across
31 Hooch
33 Punch in the stomach response
36 Shirts and blouses
37 Beetle Bailey's commander
38 ___'acte (intermission)
39 With 4-Down, modern printing fluid
40 Farm fence features
41 Prefix with -gon
42 A paramedic may look for one
44 Employ
45 Popular Ford
47 Skilled in reasoning
49 Eve's downfall
50 Lose at the bank?
51 Race unit
52 Cheap promotional trip?
58 See 30-Across

59 1973 #1 Rolling Stones hit
60 Bench site
61 Long-distance letters
62 Sailors' stories
63 Like a beach

DOWN

1 Doofus
2 Parisian pal
3 Drunk's utterance
4 See 39-Across
5 Political protest of sorts
6 Because of, with "to"
7 Successful negotiation results
8 The "E" of B.P.O.E.
9 Way to go: Abbr.
10 "Steps in Time" autobiographer
11 Pretty woman's hat?
12 Singer Bryant
13 ___ Smith, first female jockey to win a major race
18 Cross and Parker products
22 Where: Lat.
23 Musical breaks
24 ___-Detoo ("Star Wars" droid)
25 Plaything that yips?
26 Vacation spots
27 Loll
29 Gear teeth
31 Au naturel
32 Globe
34 Holy Roman emperor, 962-73
35 Swiss money
37 Talk back
38 Creepy: Var.

40 Toronto ballplayer
41 Multicar accidents
43 www.yahoo.com, e.g.
44 Pilgrimage to Mecca
45 Actress Shire
46 Besides, with "from"
47 Actor Alan
48 "The Highwayman" poet Alfred
50 Bridge builder, e.g.: Abbr.
53 Italian article
54 Actress Vardalos
55 "The Wizard of Oz" locale: Abbr.
56 Bitter ___
57 Slinky or boomerang

by Roy Leban

ACROSS

1 Variety of guitar
6 Walked (on)
10 Touches with a live wire
14 Volcanic creation
15 Part to play
16 Jacques's steady
17 Make smooth
18 Crude org.
19 Mushroom cap part
20 Hand raiser's declaration
23 ___ de guerre
24 Far from haute cuisine
25 1945 John Wayne western
27 Hand raiser's shout
32 The Louisville Lip
33 Freedom from hardship
37 "Tell Laura ___ Her" (1960 hit)
40 Burrowing insect
41 "I mean it!"
42 Leeway
44 Not healthy
45 Hand raiser's cry
50 Fountain basin feature
53 Violinist Leopold
54 Yes, to 16-Across
55 Hand raiser's request
61 Girl in Lou Bega's "Mambo No. 5"
63 "Dies ___"
64 Confident way to solve crosswords
65 Not completely closed
66 "Don't look at me!"
67 Griffin of the N.B.A.
68 Bird that "at heaven's gate sings," in Shakespeare
69 Within the hour
70 Rough tools

DOWN

1 Stock market turns
2 Parliament city
3 Not piquant
4 Take back
5 Opera with "Ave Maria"
6 ___ l'oeil
7 Part of a climber's gear
8 Couturier Cassini
9 Figures out
10 Quick sidestep
11 Protein acid
12 Person who sits in front of a cabin
13 City famously visited by Martin Luther King, Jr. in 1965
21 Motion picture angle: Abbr.
22 "Beyond the Sea" singer, 1960
26 Numbers game
27 Banshee's cry
28 "___ Enchanted" (2004 film)
29 Gasser
30 Ask for more issues
31 Beaver, e.g.
34 "Dream Children" essayist
35 Threshold
36 Peddle
38 Short biography
39 Body of good conduct
40 Hurry-scurry
43 Waifs
46 Adopt, as a pet
47 March sound
48 Harder to grasp
49 "Beverly Hills 90210" girl
50 Fable conclusion
51 Board used in "The Exorcist"
52 It was played by George Harrison
56 Suffix with sock
57 Denouncer of Caesar, 63 B.C.
58 Supports
59 Use scissors
60 Squeezes (out)
62 Torah holder

by Raymond Hamel

ACROSS

1 Tie with a cord
5 Bouts
9 Stop running
14 Nike competitor
15 A Swiss army knife has lots of them
16 Musical featuring "Little Girls"
17 Author of this puzzle's quote
19 "There you go!"
20 Text enhancer
21 Clown's prop
22 Golf cousins
23 Start of the quote
26 Miss Mexico, e.g.: Abbr.
29 Pinch
30 Move through a crowd, say
32 Quote, part 2
38 Oil-rich province
41 Northerly locale
42 Quote, part 3
44 Became rampant
45 1970 World's Fair site
48 Impertinence
49 Quote, part 4
55 Slips by
56 Big A.T.M. manufacturer
57 "Eureka!"
60 Polytheist
61 End of the quote
64 Handling badly
65 Left-handers can't play it
66 Karate skill category
67 Game with a board
68 At any time
69 Combines

DOWN

1 Alta's opposite
2 In preference to
3 Good feeling
4 Bonehead
5 Box sets?
6 Say yes
7 Prefix with graphic or metric
8 Form W-9 info: Abbr.
9 Pack rat
10 U.S. security
11 Baker of renown
12 Pastel shade
13 Get a line on?
18 Book after Galatians: Abbr.
22 Syrupy drink
23 Have second thoughts
24 Even so
25 "From Here to Eternity" island
26 Influence
27 Realtor's specialty, for short
28 Off-limits: Var.
31 Stumble
33 Two turns, maybe
34 Modern treaty violation
35 Disk contents
36 Songwriter Blackwell
37 Wetlands
39 Pixar creations
40 Lhasa ___ (dog)
43 Corrode
46 Ignite
47 Object intentionally dropped on the floor
49 Halfhearted
50 One of Donald's exes
51 Gung-ho
52 Rework
53 Smallville family
54 Grp. involved in "the Troubles"
57 Like fine wines
58 Set aside
59 Kitchen pests
61 "The Naked ___" (1960's best seller)
62 All Souls' Day mo.
63 Org. whose members use the press?

by Seth Abel

35

ACROSS

1 Holder of a lot
of hidden dirt
8 Cajun condiment
15 Basement feature,
sometimes
16 Not quite direct
17 Took some of
18 Bass offering
19 Shellback
20 Swear
22 By and by
23 Big name
in home
furnishings
25 Accommodate,
in a way
26 "The 5,000
Fingers of ___"
(1953 film
musical)
27 Emulates a wolf
29 Roller coaster
feature
31 Quintillionth:
Prefix
32 Implant deeply
34 One and only
36 Efficiency option
38 Available from,
as a product
41 Winter weather
wear with
adjustable straps
45 Eliminates as
unnecessary
46 Old Testament
figure
48 Insinuating
49 Year in
St. Gregory I's
papacy
50 Old World
grazers
52 Formerly, once
53 Duffer's obstacle
55 Isn't up
57 Bird of the
genus Corvus

58 Approach
in a hurry
60 Sure shot
62 Wearing
63 Get behind
64 Sports physicians'
concerns
65 Coty fragrance

DOWN

1 Like some egos
2 Indicate
3 Molson product
4 Something
to thank God
for: Abbr.
5 Historic
Hebrides
monastery site
6 Mississippi
senator's family
7 Gushed
8 News leader

9 Makeup course?:
Abbr.
10 "Up the Down
Staircase"
novelist Kaufman
11 Like some salts
12 Keep at steadily
13 Development
of the 1950's
14 Like some mules
21 It's not
too bright
24 Baking
by-products
28 Essential element
30 18-Across
offerers
31 Renaissance
edition of
a classic
33 Every family
has one
35 Cries of alarm

37 Optimist in
"Candide"
38 Masters
39 Good-for-nothin'
40 Record player
42 Ones who pay
attention to bills
43 "Sounds about
right to me"
44 Linking
47 They have naps
51 Knackered,
as a Brit
would say
54 Long-lasting, in
commercial names
55 Cold-cock
56 "Vic and ___" of
oldtime radio
59 Samoan staple
61 Point of "view"

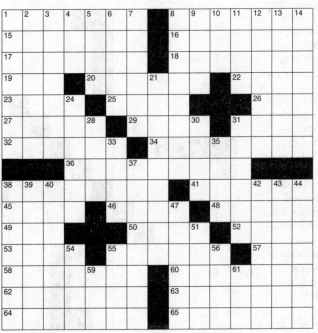

by Bob Peoples

36

ACROSS
1 Xerophyte
7 Demands
14 Surfing, say
15 Outside-the-box
16 Nation with a red-crested crane on its flag
17 Strewn
18 Good things
19 So to speak
20 Oktoberfest duds
22 Talented
23 Song that ends "Bless my homeland forever"
24 Certain charity event
25 Supporter
26 ___ special
27 Like a junker's engine
30 Dumpster lifters
31 Free-for-alls
32 Blood line
33 Resin from ancient trees
34 Dead giveaways
39 Show of absolute power
40 Corresponding
41 Regrettable occurrence
43 Hand-decorated
44 Auto part you shouldn't tamper with
45 Preshow ritual
46 "___ is knowing that your worst shot is still pretty good": golfer Johnny Miller
47 Cover
48 Matricide of Greek myth
49 Record producers

DOWN
1 Dance team
2 Like hockey sticks
3 18th-century French artist Gillot
4 Decorative threads
5 Masks are worn here
6 Oldest known form of currency
7 Surfaces
8 Became widespread
9 William of TV's "The Greatest American Hero"
10 Some Amtrak employees
11 Vessel that pumps the water it's floating in
12 Sheets used in four-color printing
13 Cashes in
15 Upmarket
21 Lubricative
24 Bridge hand assessment
26 Morning routines
27 Note on the fridge, maybe
28 Relative of a bigeye
29 Certain club reservations
30 1965 #1 hit with an exclamation point in its title
31 Family member
32 Church committee
34 What a creed is composed of
35 Pronto
36 Mystery author ___ Jackson Braun
37 Despite what you say
38 Swamp grasses
40 Secure anew
42 Ding

by Patrick Berry

ACROSS

1 Pitches four balls to
6 Cain's brother
10 Insurrectionist Turner and others
14 Not reacting chemically
15 Muse of history
16 Monogram part: Abbr.
17 Pilfer
18 Kitchen gadget that turns
20 "Faster!"
22 No great __
23 Iced tea flavoring
26 Full complement of fingers
27 Sob
30 Before, in poetry
31 Classic gas brand
34 Composer Rachmaninoff
36 Midsection muscles, for short
37 "Faster!"
40 Knight's title
41 Rat or squirrel
42 Dye containers
43 Western Indian
44 Linear, for short
45 Rope-a-dope boxer
47 Fixes
49 1960's–70's space program
52 "Faster!"
57 Cramped space
59 Rich cake
60 Primer dog
61 Sharif of film
62 Gives an audience to
63 Band with the 1988 #1 hit "Need You Tonight"
64 Monthly payment
65 Birds by sea cliffs

DOWN

1 Bit of smoke
2 Contrarians
3 Bloodsucker
4 Volcano that famously erupted in 1883
5 Acts of the Apostles writer
6 Bank holdings: Abbr.
7 Dull
8 Mozart's "a"
9 Circle
10 Daughter of a sister, perhaps
11 Ben Stiller's mother
12 Bit of business attire
13 Narrow water passage: Abbr.
19 Washed-out
21 Money for retirement
24 What a satellite may be in
25 Digs with twigs?
27 Kennel club info
28 "Son of __!"
29 Had a cow
31 __ salts
32 Luxury hotel accommodations
33 Safe
35 Mahler's "Das Lied von der __"
38 Snowman of song
39 Villain
46 Can't stand
48 Amounts in red numbers
49 Notify
50 Ship's navigation system
51 Weird
53 Norse thunder god
54 Terse directive to a chauffeur
55 Panache
56 "__ of the D'Urbervilles"
57 Popular TV police drama
58 WB competitor

by M. Francis Vuolo

ACROSS

1 Home to Honolulu
5 Sticky stuff
9 Mends, as socks
14 "The Good Earth" mother
15 Good lot size
16 "The Waste Land" poet
17 Where to find a hammer, anvil and stirrup
19 Oro y ___ (Montana's motto)
20 Charlie Rose's network
21 An Arkin
22 Ease up
23 It may be found in front of a saloon
26 Tone-___ (rapper)
27 Strong hand cleaner
31 "Doe, ___ . . ." ("The Sound of Music" lyric)
34 Queens stadium
36 6 on a phone
37 Picture-filled item often seen in a living room
41 "C'___ la vie"
42 Missing the deadline
43 Bonkers
44 Hopelessness
47 What 20-Across lacks
48 Foyer
54 Former White House pooch
57 Private eyes
58 Romance
59 Seed coverings
60 International business mantra
62 Carnival show

63 Lends a hand
64 Valuable rocks
65 Odist to a nightingale
66 McCartney played it in the Beatles
67 Top ratings

DOWN

1 That certain "something"
2 It may be airtight
3 Verb with thou
4 Sturm ___ Drang
5 Irish dialect
6 Continental divide?
7 Big ape
8 ___ capita
9 Unseat
10 Apportions
11 Inlets

12 Post-it
13 Ollie's partner in old comedy
18 Capital of Punjab province
22 Faithful
24 Staff leader?
25 First-year West Pointer
28 Melville romance
29 Before long
30 Snaillike
31 Passed with flying colors
32 Teaspoonful, maybe
33 Young newts
34 Football legend Bart
35 Where a rabbit may be hidden
38 10-point type
39 First-born

40 Twaddle
45 Small shot
46 Liqueur flavorers
47 Admission
49 Courtyards
50 Must-haves
51 Vigilant
52 Waterproof wool used for coats
53 Silt deposit
54 Word that can follow the end of 17-, 23-, 37-, 48- or 60-Across
55 "Dies ___" (liturgical poem)
56 Old Italian coin
60 Groovy
61 Twaddle

by Sarah Keller

ACROSS

1 Govt. agency since 1949
4 They may be sordid
9 Early associate of Freud
14 Popular Quaker cereal
15 Eight-ish?
16 Sporty Japanese car
17 Marceau character
18 See 33-Across
19 Intimidate, with "out"
20 Lovable curmudgeon of 1970's TV
23 Excitement
24 Treetop nibbler
28 Brownstone front
32 Play the peeping Tom
33 With 18-Across, capital of the United Arab Emirates
36 Mustang site
38 A Turner
39 Noted rehab facility
43 End in ___
44 Bucks
45 Winter Chi. clock setting
46 Lassie, for one
49 Close-knit group
51 Patella
53 Majestic
57 "The Blue Dahlia" star
61 Wing it
64 Lose one's mind
65 Loire valley product
66 Something thrown for a loop?
67 Atlantic Ten school home
68 Ike's command, once: Abbr.
69 The Dow, e.g.
70 More sound
71 Easygoing

DOWN

1 Spoil
2 Prepare eggs in a way
3 Stray place: Abbr.
4 Sole-searching, maybe?
5 Suffer
6 Shot
7 No-no: Var.
8 Armrest?
9 Current measure
10 British P.M. before Gladstone
11 Put in position
12 List ender
13 Fan noise
21 Pinafore letters
22 Laotian money
25 Swiss capital
26 Conclusion
27 Formally approve
29 Gut reaction?
30 Blue Moon of baseball
31 Contender of 1992 and 1996
33 One way to be taken
34 Be assured of
35 Handy
37 Scent
40 Air
41 Mid second-century year
42 Home of Goose Bay
47 Solitary confinement cell, in slang
48 Ring locale
50 Slithery swimmer
52 Bounces on a stick
54 Court instrument
55 Japanese dog
56 Tanglewood site, in Massachusetts
58 One of Asta's owners
59 "___ the case"
60 Nursing home staff?
61 Clay, now
62 Rather in the news
63 Cause of many trips, once

by Alan Arbesfeld

ACROSS

1 Ball
6 Not docked
10 It may be herbal
13 Blitzed
14 Sports page news
15 ___ Cenis Tunnel, in the Alps
16 Radioer's words
18 Swear words
19 Serial story line
20 Winter worry
21 Mame, for one
23 Kind of hold
24 Disney collectible
25 One who makes rounds
26 Blues alternative
27 Compass heading
29 Rescues
30 The Governator
33 How actors respond
35 2000 site
40 Build ___ (settle down)
41 Assigns
42 "Ugh!"
45 Higher degree?
47 Bull's partner
48 Grated
50 Emergency ___
52 Police blotter letters
53 Package
54 Plastic ___ Band
55 "A Woman Speaks" writer
56 Actor Morales
57 Garment with a lot of pockets
61 Muffin choice
62 S-shaped molding
63 Big name in digital software
64 Fat letters
65 Oenologist's interest
66 "The Asparagus" painter

DOWN

1 Miracle-___
2 Washroom
3 Length of a quick fight?
4 1992 site
5 Seventh in a series
6 Mystifies
7 1988 site
8 It flows through un fleuve
9 Russia's ___ Republic
10 Precisely
11 Uncut
12 With 42-Down, 2004 site
15 1976 site
17 Eagles div.
22 Stretch out
26 Flier to Helsinki
28 Naval rank: Abbr.
31 You can see right through them
32 Change from bland to blond?
34 Loop group: Abbr.
36 Figure on an ancient Egyptian headband
37 Visit briefly, as someone who's sick
38 "I don't believe this!"
39 Show curiosity
42 See 12-Down
43 1996 Ron Howard thriller
44 Jack Nicholson has three
46 Home run, in baseball slang
49 Undercover cop, maybe
51 Overly
58 Francis Bacon said it "will not be defied"
59 Popular cooking spray
60 Stiffen

by David J. Kahn

ACROSS

1 Edelweiss source
5 First name at Woodstock
9 "That really happened!"
14 Give rise to
15 National competitor
16 Harped
17 Bridge words
18 Gubernatorial right
19 À la King
20 Ship damaged in the attack on Pearl Harbor
22 Fact finder, say
24 Islamic Republic Day observer
25 Follower of a wondrous feat
27 "Mystic River" co-star, 2003
28 Boxing historian Fleischer
29 Upright relatives
32 Bill of Rights subj.
33 Political symbol
35 Political symbol
37 33- or 35-Across?
39 Military shell thrower
41 Popular furry 1980's toy
44 1990 Hollywood autobiography subtitled "My Story"
45 Took up
47 1988 purchaser of Motown
48 Gospel singer Winans
50 Zip
51 Collars may cover them
53 Naive

55 Special Forces wear
56 55-Across's lacks
57 Reliever's triumph
60 Tough test
61 Olympics array
62 Quaint outburst
63 Parcel
64 Hot time in Argentina
65 Film, in Variety-speak
66 Father of Harmonia

DOWN

1 Sans sense
2 Bounteous
3 A doctor may open one
4 Driver's choice
5 Site of a famed fossil find

6 It may be added to impress
7 "Good Will Hunting" setting, briefly
8 King Mark's bride
9 Noodle product?
10 Weenie
11 He played a monocled colonel in a sitcom
12 Legal heir, at times
13 One way to issue a warning
21 Kitchen sink sight
23 Grovel
25 Causing squinting, perhaps
26 Settler in a drugstore
30 Regulars
31 Unnamed source

34 Way to stand
36 Nail
38 Dog of literature
39 À la King
40 Engulfed
42 Transparency
43 Scraps in the backwoods
46 Loafer attachment
49 One known for stick-to-it-iveness?
52 Dining room drawer
54 Brand with a tiger slogan
55 Inn inventory
58 Biographical bit
59 Delivery aid

by Harvey Estes

ACROSS

1 Fill
5 Puppets
15 Blockage
16 Question from the back seat
17 Excitedly
18 Napery
19 Decrease the production (of)
21 Beginning of time?
22 Fancy
23 Fire extinguishers
25 Foes of the Seminoles
27 3.7×10 to the 10th power disintegrations per second, to a physicist
28 Certain Arab
29 Ideal match, it's said, for a Cabernet Sauvignon
33 Kind of seat
34 Break time, often
35 Buddy, in slang
36 Wasn't generous with
39 Group belonging to the same rank
41 Top spot?
42 Give
43 1997 Stallone film
46 Thomas Mann novella "___ Kröger"
47 "I'm gone"
48 Flip over
51 Temporary lodging
54 1950's–60's TV horse
55 Having little support
56 Sailing along
57 Good bettors follow it
58 Shockingly bright

DOWN

1 Cozenage
2 Eukaryotic organism
3 Went faster than by foot, say
4 Exhorted
5 Mums
6 Wipe
7 Bills
8 Symbol of Minerva
9 It's often fixed
10 Super Bowl champs of 2000
11 Not laid on thick
12 She played Irene in "Me, Myself & Irene"
13 Backward
14 Proceeds
20 Romance author Foster
23 Longtime Leonard foe
24 Its nickname is "Family City, U.S.A."
25 A lot
26 Crazily
27 Woodskin, e.g.
29 Made over
30 Feature of good design
31 Start of a show
32 Biting
34 It has a forked tail
37 Foulness
38 Robert Burns, the ___ Bard
39 Galilee town in John 2:1
40 Follower and then some
42 Obtain
43 Family heads
44 Loathing
45 Noted Italian marble
46 "Careless Hands" crooner, 1949
48 Show of amusement
49 Wafers-and-creme treat
50 Baseball's first $1 million/year player
52 Topper
53 "Olé ___" (1976 rock album)

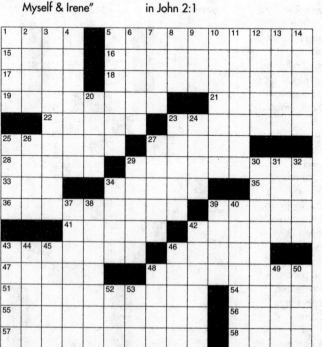

by Joe DiPietro

ACROSS

1 Poi source
5 "The Thin Man" dog
9 Rum-soaked cakes
14 Stench
15 Where an honoree may sit
16 Friend, south of the border
17 Rocket scientist's employer
18 Prefix with potent
19 Alpine song
20 Not much
23 ___ glance (quickly)
24 Center of activity
25 Grammys, e.g.
29 Tip for a ballerina
31 Aide: Abbr.
35 Funnel-shaped
36 Craze
38 Hurry
39 Activities that generate no money
42 Surgery spots, for short
43 Indians of New York
44 Jack who ate no fat
45 Seeded loaves
47 Dog-tag wearers, briefly
48 Choirs may stand on them
49 Overly
51 Loser to D.D.E. twice
52 Boatswains, e.g.
59 R-rated, say
61 Poker payment
62 Confess
63 Tutu material
64 Rude look
65 Peru's capital
66 Back tooth
67 Slips
68 Fizzless, as a soft drink

DOWN

1 Cargo weights
2 Sandler of "Big Daddy"
3 Painter Bonheur
4 Face-to-face exam
5 Takes as one's own
6 Pago Pago's land
7 Salon application
8 Where Nepal is
9 Louisiana waterway
10 Microscopic organism
11 Bridge declarations
12 Questionnaire datum
13 Note after fa
21 Scottish beau
22 "A League of ___ Own" (1992 comedy)
25 Cast member
26 "What, me ___?"
27 Liqueur flavorer
28 Speed (up)
29 Blackmailer's evidence
30 Burden
32 English county
33 Ravi Shankar's instrument
34 Checkups
36 1052, in a proclamation
37 St. Francis' birthplace
40 Lingo
41 Raises
46 "A Streetcar Named Desire" woman
48 Directs (to)
50 Stream bank cavorter
51 "___ you" ("You go first")
52 Clout
53 Connecticut campus
54 Unique individual
55 Ranch newborn
56 Diabolical
57 Capital south of Venezia
58 Whack
59 Bank amenity, for short
60 Pair

by Joy C. Frank

44

ACROSS

1. ___ the Red
5. Fragrant blossom
10. "Right on!"
14. Woodworking groove
15. Excitedly
16. Stack
17. He wrote "Utopia" in an ancient language
19. Yard sale tag
20. Partner of "ifs" and "ands"
21. Arterial trunks
23. Do a favor
26. Be charitable
28. Tilted
29. Oxidize
30. A.A.A. suggestion: Abbr.
33. Office stamp
34. Better halves
35. Disney Store item
36. "How Sweet ___"
37. Mocks
38. Something that shouldn't be left hanging
39. Twilight time to a poet
40. More immense
41. Rear
42. TV prog. with a different host each week
43. Cupid's counterpart
44. Author Lee
45. Inner circle member
47. Keats and others
48. Hogan dweller
50. Seed cover
51. Oscar winner Guinness
52. Blind poet who often wrote in an ancient language
58. Desertlike
59. Gladden
60. Dust Bowl refugee
61. Pianist Dame Myra
62. Dravidian language
63. ___ contendere

DOWN

1. Summer hrs. in N.J.
2. Cheer
3. Life-changing statement
4. Farm vehicles
5. Endured
6. Many P.C.'s
7. London lav
8. Vacuum's lack
9. Purifies
10. Not close
11. He taught an ancient language in film
12. Old London Magazine essayist
13. Celebrated Prohibition-era lawman
18. Tool with a cross handle
22. Feedbag feed
23. "Golden" things
24. Vanquished
25. What 17- and 52-Across and 11-Down all were
26. Curtain
27. North Carolina's ___ Banks
31. Some china
32. Church V.I.P.'s
34. Myopic cartoon character
37. Certain Boeing
38. Church music maker
40. Muslim pilgrimage
41. Arm bones
44. Spam producer
46. Adds punch to, as punch
48. Bygone auto
49. Toward shelter
50. Not pro
53. Commercial suffix with Motor
54. Biblical ark passenger
55. Ref's decision
56. 3-in-One product
57. "The Matrix" role

by Gene Newman

45

ACROSS

1 Drug buster
5 Eight furlongs
9 Fishermen's pailfuls
14 1998 Sarah McLachlan hit
15 Double agent Aldrich
16 Sleep disorder
17 Fake cover stories
19 "Bad" for "good," e.g.
20 Dress with a flare
21 Stephen Foster classic
23 Back of the boat
25 Key of Beethoven's Symphony No. 7: Abbr.
27 Attacked with zeal
28 Not nerdy
30 Bikini blast, briefly
32 Stumblers' sounds
33 Get a program on the radio
35 Mars explorer
37 Homeric epic
38 Familiar Olympics chant
39 King protectors
43 Watch
45 Catch between bases, say
46 K.C.-to-Little Rock direction
48 Surveyors' calculations
50 ___ Stanley Gardner
51 Grand
53 Equine quipster
55 Airline to Amsterdam
56 Hermit
58 Omnium-gatherums
60 Running wild
61 Shocked response in conversation
65 Reaches over
66 Move, in Realtor-speak
67 Easy gait
68 "Roots" writer
69 Once, once upon a time
70 Hightailed it

DOWN

1 Get the drop on
2 Stir
3 Tubes on the table
4 Being the reason for
5 Best bro
6 Pooped person's plaint
7 Pacific ring
8 "Happy Motoring" company
9 Méphistophélès player in "Faust"
10 Valedictorian's feat, perhaps
11 Comparatively cockamamie
12 Court contest
13 "Contact" astronomer
18 ___ Fail (Irish coronation stone)
22 Modern viewer's option, briefly
23 When Hamlet sees his father's ghost
24 Cager's offense
26 Destination for many pilgrims
29 "Three's a crowd"
31 March master
34 Exiled Amin
36 Org. concerned with PCB's
38 Onetime TWA rival
40 Place with sawdust
41 Zero
42 Leaf holder
44 Gallivants
45 J. Alfred Prufrock poet
46 Himalayan guide
47 Mixer
49 Wakeup calls
51 Riffraff
52 Cracked
54 Performed
57 Fictional Jane
59 Barn birds
62 Donne's "done"
63 Big brute
64 Newsman Koppel

by Nancy Salomon and Levi Denham

46

ACROSS

1 Fair-sized garden
5 Tater
9 Cue user
14 "Mon ___!"
15 Garr of film
16 Carrying out the garbage, e.g.
17 Impugn
19 "My Friend" of 1950's TV and others
20 What Satan gets from poison ivy?
22 With 45-Across, book title with a hint to this puzzle's theme
24 Chinese dynasty of 2,000 years ago
25 Underground facility
26 Foreshadowed
27 Like some lines
29 G.I.'s address
30 Orderly phrase that can follow one, two or three
34 Money earned by a hospital worker?
39 When there may be censorship
40 New Deal agcy.
42 Corps member
45 See 22-Across
47 Spray target
48 Big name in ISP's
51 "Aieeeee!," e.g.
52 Donation for crackpots?
55 Film director Kenton and others
56 Pertaining to the lower skull bone
59 Hardly accepting
60 Truckful
61 Architect Saarinen
62 Clipped
63 Alternatively
64 Vitamin amts.

DOWN

1 Word on a dipstick
2 Year in Trajan's reign
3 Used as a chair
4 Cheat, slangily
5 They may be Irish
6 Prefix with cab
7 "Spenser: For Hire" star
8 Bears Hall-of-Famer Mike
9 It has a low pH
10 Name
11 Wren, for one
12 Answer provider
13 Like work horses, often
18 Matting material
21 Salad leaf
22 I.B.F. rival
23 Kachina doll maker
28 Cockney's residence
30 State of lateness
31 Blaster
32 Uris hero ___ Ben Canaan
33 Pro ___
35 Majorettes, e.g.
36 Suffix with Euclid
37 Like some stocks
38 Second planet past Merkur
41 In perfect condition
42 Product introduced in 1908 "for the great multitude"
43 Renée of silents
44 Painting aid
45 Trounce
46 More pretentious
49 "___ Mio"
50 Rank above maj.
51 Sarcastic
53 "___ sow . . ."
54 Wood sorrels
57 Coach Parseghian
58 ___ Alamitos, Calif.

by Ed Early

ACROSS

1 Like some doughnuts
16 It'll do your heart good
17 They have to listen
18 Letters of royalty
19 Doesn't get everything one wants
20 Mushroom part
21 Those in La Mancha
23 Breeds
24 Runner's goal
25 Chief Justice in the Dred Scott case
27 Some are odd: Abbr.
28 Stuff in a closet
29 Blood pressure readings
31 Pulled tight
32 They may be draining
33 Counter's start
34 They're fed at curbside
37 War game
41 Unearthly
42 Italian pronoun
43 One who made Ulysses fit to be tied
44 Pitcher Maglie and others
45 Emulates a 43-Across
47 Prefix with language
48 Radar, e.g.: Abbr.
49 Cloak
51 Harris of Hollywood
52 Choice words
55 One with a poll position?
56 Classic Frank Loesser song from a 1950 musical

DOWN

1 Distinguishing marks
2 Court no-no, usually
3 "Father Murphy" extras
4 Simple sack
5 Eastern ties
6 Video game allotment
7 Thinner components
8 Where drammi are performed
9 Crows
10 Yields
11 ". . . ___ it me?"
12 Rare driving result
13 They inspired Andy Warhol
14 Coop flier
15 Hysteria area
22 Parlor fixtures
24 1960's falsetto singer
26 Colloquial possessive
28 Actress Headey and others
30 Abbr. for dumbbells
31 Thrice: Lat.
33 Tchotchke holders
34 It may run in the rain
35 Ran out
36 Farmer's fieldwork
37 Open
38 Taker of a religious vow
39 Pay someone back
40 Watching
42 Stamped out, in a way
45 Longtime Chicago maestro
46 C.D. source
49 Latin quarters
50 Composition of some beds
53 Lacking value
54 Boy whose name is repeated in a nursery rhyme

by Harvey Estes

48

ACROSS

1 Old-time poacher deterrents
9 Doesn't do enough
15 "That was the last straw!"
16 Ready to be engaged
17 Heat shield location
18 Disturbed the peace
19 Overdrawn
20 Wife to José
21 It's sold in sticks
22 Jets player whose jersey #12 was retired
24 Rest
25 "Drat!"
27 Sailor's punishment
28 Funny __ (2003 Derby winner)
29 Addressed flippantly
31 Hang-ups
33 Some people can wiggle them
35 Another name for Cupid
36 Singer with the 1994 #1 hit "Stay"
40 Where people get loaded on trains
44 Building block
45 The Sudanese Republic, today
47 He said "The only alternative to coexistence is co-destruction"
48 Sportscaster Allen
49 Duds
51 Takes a powder
52 Female patron saint of Ireland
54 Dismissive remark
56 Alchemic knowledge
57 One of Rome's seven hills
58 Examine
59 What Vito Corleone's company imported
60 Hard to please
61 Stand in the great hall?

DOWN

1 Big wheel's entourage
2 L. M. Montgomery book "Anne of __"
3 Empty __
4 A bad situation, slangily
5 People
6 Trim
7 __ gland (melatonin secreter)
8 Longtime beau of Oprah
9 Big digit?
10 Turnover
11 Restaurant chain, for short
12 Process by which one cell becomes two
13 Officiate
14 Knocks out
23 Perplexed
26 Part of a dollar bill
28 Spots connections between
30 Caravan carrier
32 Gray-spotted horse
34 Clothing line?
36 Lower back pain
37 Mistaken
38 Element used to make semiconductors
39 Two-layered candy
41 Certain two-wheeler
42 Neighbor of Georgia
43 __ Long, Louisiana senator, 1948–87
46 Gulp
49 Makeup item
50 100%
53 Yielded
55 Yield

by Patrick Berry

ACROSS

1 Tree that people carve their initials in
6 Pepper's partner
10 Author Dinesen
14 Stevenson of 1950's politics
15 Dunkable cookie
16 Plot parcel
17 "Dee-licious!"
19 Alum
20 Carson's predecessor on "The Tonight Show"
21 Surgeon's outfit
23 Play parts
26 Goes to sleep, with "off"
29 Skirt lines
30 Bangkok native
31 Like snow after a blizzard, perhaps
33 Corrosions
35 Eyelid problem
36 Spanish aunt
39 Crying
42 Evangeline or Anna Karenina, e.g.
44 What candles sometimes represent
45 "Very funny!"
47 Animal nose
48 Show biz parent
52 Go left or right
53 Petri dish filler
54 Where the Himalayas are
55 Not in port
56 Main arteries
58 Den
60 High spirits
61 "Dee-licious!"
67 Fanny
68 Certain woodwind
69 Pitcher Martínez
70 Painting and sculpting, e.g.
71 Yards advanced
72 Animal in a roundup

DOWN

1 San Francisco/Oakland separator
2 School's Web site address ender
3 Shade tree
4 Where a tent is pitched
5 "Howdy!"
6 Grow sick of
7 Quarterback's asset
8 Moon lander, for short
9 Santa's sackful
10 "Amen!"
11 "Dee-licious!"
12 Saudis and Iraqis
13 Classic sneakers
18 American, abroad
22 Bar "where everybody knows your name"
23 Skylit lobbies
24 Newswoman Connie
25 "Dee-licious!"
27 ___ Moines
28 Genesis son
32 Color, as an Easter egg
34 African desert
37 Get used (to)
38 MetLife competitor
40 Scandal sheet
41 Where the Mets can be met
43 Perfectly precise
46 Mornings, briefly
49 Spuds
50 Some Texas tycoons
51 "Just the facts, ___"
53 One who hears "You've got mail"
56 Taj Mahal site
57 Urban haze
59 Little devils
62 Entrepreneur's deg.
63 "Who, me?"
64 "___ to Joy"
65 Mine find
66 "Le Coq ___"

by Nancy Salomon and Kyle Mahowald

ACROSS

1 Sharp-eyed raptor
6 Kid's getaway
10 Military level
14 Lamebrain
15 Off base illegally
16 "Garfield" dog
17 "The Godfather" actor's reputation?
19 Umpteen
20 UFO fliers
21 Novelist Zane
22 River under London Bridge, once
24 Alfalfa, Spanky and others
26 Tibia's place
27 Christian pop singer Grant
28 Camera-friendly events
32 Cheap jewelry
35 Rapunzel's abundance
36 Off-key, in a way
37 Garage occupant
38 "It ain't over till it's over" speaker
39 Gawk at
40 Beach sidler
41 New York City's ___ River
42 Comprehend
43 Arrange in columns
45 Old French coin
46 Rolling in the dough
47 Stops talking suddenly
51 Pants measure
54 Soccer success
55 Expert
56 Fan club's honoree
57 U2 singer's journey?
60 Indian tourist site
61 River to the Caspian
62 Lecture jottings
63 Posterior
64 Kittens' cries
65 Dress to kill, with "up"

DOWN

1 Fireplace glower
2 Line from the heart
3 Wimbledon court surface
4 Actor Chaney
5 Final stage, in chess
6 Yuletide sweets
7 On vacation
8 S.U.V. "chauffeur," maybe
9 Overabundance
10 Actor Ray's discussion group?
11 First mate?
12 "The Whole ___ Yards"
13 Florida islets
18 Air France destination
23 Chart topper
25 Roman statesman's thieving foe?
26 Tank top, e.g.
28 Analyze, as a sentence
29 Gymnast Korbut
30 Buddies
31 Put one's foot down?
32 Hostilities ender
33 Subtle glow
34 Attempt
35 Shrubby tract
38 Lauderdale loafer
42 Cooperate (with)
44 Soused
45 Pole or Bulgarian
47 Puts on ice
48 Petty quarrels
49 More than suggests
50 Metrical verse
51 Tall tale teller
52 Upper hand
53 Writer Ephron
54 Chew like a rat
58 Vein contents
59 "___ rang?"

by Lynn Lempel

Note: Each of the three theme answers below (20-, 36- and 54-Across) can be clued with the same three letters.

ACROSS

1 Chick on the piano
6 P.D.Q. in the I.C.U.
10 Casing
14 Ph.D. hurdle
15 Part of "S.N.L."
16 Narrow way
17 Try to bite
18 Mental flash
19 Aboard
20 [See instructions]
23 Flamenco shout
24 Sushi selection
25 Comb stopper
27 Harangues
30 Toward the tail
32 Copacabana site
33 Youth
34 Dedicated lines?
35 Kennel sound
36 [See instructions]
41 Leave the scene
42 Satisfy the munchies
43 50-50, e.g.
44 Old discs
45 Orthodontist, for one: Abbr.
46 Calls the shots
50 Words of assistance
52 Sidekick
53 Cry of insight
54 [See instructions]
59 Cork's country
60 Confess
61 Camel caravan's stop-off
62 Tend the sauce
63 Victory goddess
64 Advil alternative
65 Caribbean and others
66 Rock radio pioneer Freed
67 Administered medicine

DOWN

1 Swindle
2 Yankee opponent
3 Cousin of an épée
4 Zing
5 Vino region
6 Covers with gunk
7 Kind of basin
8 State firmly
9 Sign of sorrow
10 "Wake of the Ferry" painter
11 Pocket protector?
12 Cabinet post since 1849
13 Opposite of paleo-
21 Ribbed
22 Follower's suffix
26 Barn section
28 Heaps
29 Letter from Greece
30 Flap
31 Productive
34 Frequently, in verse
35 "Whoopee!"
36 Healthy
37 Speed up
38 Ornamental vine: Var.
39 "__ Kapital"
40 What a person may become when kneeling
45 Society newbie
46 Obscure
47 Political movements
48 Prosper
49 Got fresh with
51 Mike who played Austin Powers
52 Lawrence Welk specialty
55 Sicilian hothead?
56 Come up short
57 Loathsome person
58 Sign of sanctity
59 Double curve

by Richard Silvestri

ACROSS

1 Prevalent
5 ___ & Whitney (aircraft engine manufacturer)
10 Flake material
14 Book of the Book of Mormon
15 Nouveau ___
16 College in New Rochelle, N.Y.
17 Barks up the wrong tree
18 Rhode Island, with "the"
20 See 34-, 42- and 55-Across
22 Rakes in
23 Mme., across the Pyrenees
24 Subj. of a 1984 Stephen Ambrose political biography
25 Daycare charge
29 Speed demon
34 19th-century writer/lecturer who advocated 20-Across
38 Like "der," in Ger.
40 "Lorna ___"
41 Inspirer
42 19th-century dress reformer who advocated 20-Across
45 Attacks
46 Trollope's "Lady ___"
47 It may give you a charge
50 Fed. bureau with agents
53 Walk down the aisle?
55 19th-century author/hymnist who advocated 20-Across

60 Needle holder
62 Rear end
63 Retained
64 It has bands with music
65 Morales of "N.Y.P.D. Blue"
66 Division preposition
67 Idyllic spots
68 Proceed

DOWN

1 Passed through, as a rope
2 Encroachment
3 Strongholds
4 German steel city
5 Univ. V.I.P.
6 Wealthy, in Juárez
7 Whiz of a tennis server
8 Détentes
9 ___ sax
10 Snack
11 Flecked horse
12 Six-footer
13 Dundee denial
19 Sassy
21 Grounded jets
26 When said three times, "et cetera"
27 Tree or door feature
28 Dreaded virus
30 "Alas!"
31 Place to get hitched, perhaps
32 Dash lengths
33 Certain whiskey
35 Bruins home, for short
36 Like many a quip: Abbr.
37 "Open all night" sign, maybe
38 ___-jongg

39 Grp. with a famous journal
43 Author Calvino
44 Antarctica's Queen ___ Mountains
48 "Seinfeld" character
49 Fearful
51 Feline in un jardin zoologique
52 Measure of capacitance
54 Nag
55 Elbow hard
56 Word processor command
57 Baseballer Boggs
58 Neat as ___
59 Fraternity letters
60 ___ Beta Kappa
61 Setter

by Stella Daily and Bruce Venzke

ACROSS

1 Bar stools, e.g.
8 Like show horses
15 For fun
16 Early art supplier
17 Basketball Hall-of-Famer Dick, who played for the 1950's Knicks
18 Former British royal house
19 Prominent schnauzer feature
20 Chap
21 Quarter of M
22 Wet bar?
23 Cartoon character whose first name is Quincy
26 The pit
27 Refreshers
31 Hungry person's hyperbole
34 Order of business?
35 Communication ender
36 Cheers
37 Do
38 Tightens, as a belt
39 Ones yelling 36-Across
40 "Dude," in Kingston
41 Marigolds, e.g.
45 Mars Bars, e.g.
49 Tim'rous one, to Burns
50 Where to spend kroons
51 Setting for Longfellow's "The Wreck of the Hesperus"
52 Ill-used
53 Celeb-to-be
54 Light, with "to"

DOWN

1 Apple, to a botanist
2 Suffix with consist
3 It may make your face red
4 Two-door closed cars with back seats
5 Ash, e.g.
6 Morris who directed "Fog of War"
7 Bias
8 One quarter, maybe
9 Skipper's run
10 Supermarket chain
11 P.S. on an invitation
12 Serenader's sentiment
13 Zeno's home
14 Sew up
22 Ushers
23 It has little meaning
24 Get ___ reception
25 Pig out
26 Miraculous
27 Dozing
28 Eagerness
29 False front?
30 Some Rockefeller Center murals
32 Write quickly
33 Haunt
39 Calamitous
40 ___ Sharett, Israel's first foreign minister, 1949–56
41 Kid's recitation
42 How Scotch may be served
43 Wine area
44 One with ulterior motives
45 Promontory
46 Con
47 Bank
48 "The Sweetest Taboo" singer, 1985

by Manny Nosowsky

ACROSS

1 Kind of engr.
5 Quiverful, e.g.
10 Cudgel
14 String of numbers?
15 Col. Klink's secretary
16 Brutus's blood vessel
17 It's full of cuts
19 Lift innovator
20 Green shade
21 Editor's request
23 One may carry off carrion
25 Pseudologue
26 Europeans, to colonial Indians
29 Bagatelles
33 Lew Wallace's "Ben-Hur: ___ of the Christ"
34 Position
35 Dr.'s order
36 It may be in a split
39 Physics 12-Down
40 Blois is on it
41 1953 Louis L'Amour novel
42 Follower
44 Conversation opener
45 It'll give you the edge
46 Economizes, with "down"
48 Boilerplate word
51 Like some kings
55 Rods and such
56 Sequin alternative
58 Trough site
59 Gone, in a way
60 Degas detail
61 African antelope
62 Some gowns
63 Wedding couple?

DOWN

1 N.Y.C. tourist attraction
2 Peak stat.
3 Giorgio's greeting
4 It may have an alarm rating
5 Window shopper's purchase?
6 Marsh fisher
7 Forest ranger
8 "Happy Days Are Here Again" composer
9 Indicator of success in life, to a palmist
10 "Songs My Mother Taught Me" composer
11 It's no longer working
12 See 39-Across
13 Kind of pay or path
18 Big makeup maker
22 Porch item
24 Arrays
26 On disk, say
27 Combat producer
28 Is very burdensome
30 Run for the money
31 Reciprocity
32 One who says a lot?
34 Make a wake
37 Like a basset
38 "The Blessed Damozel" poet
43 Learning center
44 Department store section
47 Company avoider
48 Vincent van Gogh's brother
49 Sense, in a way
50 Alternative to Chinese or Indian
52 Common contraction
53 Inner opening?
54 Evan S. Connell's "___ lo Volt!"
57 Drafter of the Meiji constitution

by Dana Motley

ACROSS

1 Tow
5 From County Clare, e.g.
10 ___ pet (onetime fad item)
14 "The Thin Man" pooch
15 Off-limits
16 "Crazy" bird
17 Manual transmission
19 "What've you been ___?"
20 Politely
21 High-spirited horse
23 Swap
24 From one side to the other
26 Shade of beige
28 Warwick who sang "Walk On By"
32 Tree branch
36 Makes a row in a garden, say
38 "Hasta la vista!"
39 Operatic solo
40 Academy Award
42 Fighting, often with "again"
43 Goes off on a mad tangent
45 With 22-Down, Korea's location
46 Bone-dry
47 Moose or mouse
49 Perlman of "Cheers"
51 Upstate New York city famous for silverware
53 Twinkie's filling
58 Versatile legume
61 Entraps
62 Jai ___
63 Lakeshore rental, perhaps
66 Lass

67 Between, en français
68 Taking a break from work
69 One of two wives of Henry VIII
70 Hem again
71 Loch ___ monster

DOWN

1 Lacks, quickly
2 Up and about
3 Ancient city NW of Carthage
4 Tied, as shoes
5 ___-bitsy
6 Shout from the bleachers
7 There: Lat.
8 Until now
9 Souped-up car
10 Standard drink mixers

11 Arizona tribe
12 Tiny amount
13 Shortly
18 Swiss artist Paul ___
22 See 45-Across
24 Came up
25 What a TV host reads from
27 Funnywoman Margaret
29 Evening, in ads
30 Dark film genre, informally
31 Villa d'___
32 "___ Croft Tomb Raider" (2001 film)
33 Tehran's land
34 Prefix with skirt or series
35 Transportation for the Dynamic Duo

37 Bird's name in "Peter and the Wolf"
41 Numbered rd.
44 Of sound mind
48 Frog, at times
50 Unappealing skin condition
52 Idiotic
54 1990's Israeli P.M.
55 Wear away
56 Breakfast, lunch and dinner
57 Kefauver of 1950's politics
58 The "Star Wars" trilogy, for one
59 Actress Lena
60 Folksy tale
61 Whole bunch
64 Alcoholic's woe
65 Rapper Dr. ___

by Jeffrey Harris

56

ACROSS

1 New stable arrival
5 Wrigley team
9 Beginning
14 Old Dodge model
15 Pronto!
16 Captain Nemo's creator
17 Jared of "Panic Room"
18 "A ___ formality!"
19 Chip away at
20 Winter accessory
23 Up to, in ads
24 Coll., e.g.
25 However, informally
28 Caffeine source for many
33 Learn about
35 The whole shebang
36 Forest canine
38 Sailing hazards
41 Geo. W. Bush has one
42 Artfully dodge
43 Simple door fastener
46 Price word
47 Black-and-orange songbird
48 Polite drivers, at merges
51 Columbia Univ. locale
52 Something to shuck
54 ___ de Cologne
55 What the ends of 20-, 36- and 43-Across suggest
61 Language of India
64 Actress Malone
65 Tea time, perhaps
66 French farewell
67 Wide-eyed
68 Book after II Chronicles
69 1692 witch trials city
70 Fine-tune
71 For fear that

DOWN

1 Arlo Guthrie's genre
2 Spilled salt, say
3 Pro's foe
4 Ray of "GoodFellas"
5 The Kennedy years, figuratively
6 Played for a sap
7 3 Musketeers units
8 Eyeglasses, informally
9 "Yoo-hoo!"
10 Soft ball material
11 Sellout indicator
12 Cut short
13 Pigskin prop
21 Part of three-in-a-row
22 Yearn (for)
25 Minstrel show group
26 Player in extra-point attempts
27 Job seekers' good news
28 Graphite element
29 Legendary Mrs. who owned a cow
30 Frock wearer
31 Arm or leg
32 Perth ___, N.J.
34 Piercing tool
37 Java neighbor
39 To's partner
40 Element #34
44 First wife of Jacob
45 Like many MTV viewers
49 Slip behind
50 Camper's bag
53 Indian prince
55 ___ fixe (obsession)
56 Toy block maker
57 Get ___ the ground floor
58 Gooey stuff
59 Sharer's word
60 "Dang!"
61 Is afflicted with
62 Actress Lupino
63 Zip

by Nancy Kavanaugh

ACROSS

1 Holiday visitor, maybe
6 Sporty car, for short
10 Plum Nascar position
14 Western necktie?
15 Crashing sort
16 Hera's mother
17 Knew
20 Dish cooked in a pot
21 Trim, in a way
22 Key material
23 Ludwig Mies van der ___
25 Gospel writer
27 New
33 Prefix with arthritis
34 Forum greeting
35 Brought up
37 Mao's successor
38 Alistair who wrote "Ice Station Zebra"
42 Put away
43 D.C. baseballers
45 See 27-Down
46 Derby place
48 Nu
52 Rough tool
53 Kitchen flooring, for short
54 Scarecrow's composition
57 Viking's deity
59 Bubble wrap sounds
63 Gnu
66 Feels punk
67 Peace Nobelist Ducommun
68 2000 N.B.A. M.V.P.
69 Spymaster's worry
70 Rx amts.
71 Famous "hostess with the mostest"

DOWN

1 Poop
2 Seasonal air
3 Veg out
4 Fertility goddess
5 Chinese dynasty name
6 Homes
7 Like a Hail Mary pass
8 Woodstock phenomenon
9 1950's political initials
10 Poor Richard's Almanack item
11 "You gotta be kidding!"
12 Wolf's look
13 "Duck soup!"
18 Classic soft drink
19 Triathlete's need
24 Baseball's Blue Moon
26 Iris's place
27 With 45-Across, noted Arctic explorer
28 Bar order, with "the"
29 ___ Department
30 Novelist Carr
31 Wipe out
32 Dry out, informally
36 Prefix with god
39 Bellicose god
40 HOV lane users
41 It's inert
44 Berlin boulevard
47 Barbecuer's buy
49 Fancy marbles
50 Skips over
51 50's car features
54 Ponzi scheme, e.g.
55 Cream was one
56 Frank holder
58 Socially challenged sort
60 Reveals, in verse
61 Survey map
62 Ward of the screen
64 Rainy
65 Author Clancy

by Jim Conklin

ACROSS

1 Tumbler's need
4 Palme of Sweden
8 Airport parking area
13 Got down
14 Major exporter of coconut oil
16 Crackers
17 Silver on the silver screen
18 With 20- and 55-Across, description of 60-Across
20 See 18-Across
22 Rig
23 Bean products?
24 Bite lightly into
28 Wife of Osiris
32 Place for a miss
36 Hide-hair link
38 News for the Wall St. Journal
39 "Is that ___?"
40 Investigator's question
41 Team in 1969 headlines
45 Ginsberg classic
46 Pizazz
47 Montreal university
51 Deli wares
55 See 18-Across
60 Western tourist attraction
61 Menu phrase
62 Knocked down
63 Give access to
64 Jiffy
65 Defeatist's words
66 Wisconsin natives
67 Put to the test

DOWN

1 Teammate of Mantle
2 Observe Yom Kippur
3 Brunch time, for some
4 Bone: Prefix
5 Retreat
6 Bygone science magazine
7 Nickname for San Francisco
8 Beginning
9 Do a fraternity prank, maybe
10 Much more than a snicker
11 For ___ (on this occasion)
12 Bill ___, the Science Guy
15 "When I was ___ . . ."
19 Lamb's dam
21 Sweeper's target?
25 "___ to please"
26 Insect stage
27 Completely
29 Embroiders a bit
30 Suffix with book
31 Place for shoats
32 Suds
33 Lingo
34 "___ Own" (song from "Les Miz")
35 December air
36 Extreme
37 "Really, now!"
42 Draws
43 Vacation spots
44 Kind of paper
48 ___ Triomphe
49 Letters on a brandy bottle
50 Popular shaver
52 It helps your dough grow
53 One on a conger line?
54 Keach who played Mike Hammer on TV
55 One in a mare's nest?
56 Colorless liqueur
57 Canzone melody
58 Stoltz of "Pulp Fiction"
59 Retired fliers
60 When many banks have extra hrs.

by David J. Kahn

ACROSS

1 Playfully roguish
5 One up
11 Mountain pass
14 Owner of the Y?
15 Saint said to have been martyred by Huns
16 Ex of Mickey
17 Ready to get drunk, perhaps
18 Sports film that was a 2003 Best Picture nominee
20 Like a smoker
21 Pollute, say
22 Winner of nine golf majors
23 Tough
25 Fox's relative
27 Remote choice
28 Like retirees
30 Nottingham nursery needs
32 Article written by Kant
33 Running things in a bar
35 In things
36 Oddball
38 Ward of the screen
41 Like many hearths
42 Court people, for short
45 Is faithful (to)
47 Life saver
49 Twin
50 Code word
52 Shake, to some
53 It's divided into 24 books
55 Mend
57 Berth place
58 Novel featuring the madam Dora Flood
60 A famous Amos

61 Took the cake, say
62 Richard's "On Your Toes" collaborator
63 Sister on "The Waltons"
64 Marshaled
65 Unfortunate things to have to count
66 Homes in the woods

DOWN

1 Rolled up
2 Old bar material
3 One working on the spot?
4 Person who won't commit
5 Like a fox
6 Country statistic

7 Bygone leaders
8 Abolitionist Harriet
9 Certain Ivy Leaguer
10 Dermal development
11 "la Orana Maria" painter
12 Kept one's nose in the air?
13 Glib quality
19 Drive
24 Lose the freshness of youth
26 Be out briefly?
29 Corporate inits. since 1924
31 Talking up?
34 Retiree server: Abbr.
36 "Riverdance" composer Bill

37 Something to believe in
38 Extreme
39 Admire to a fault
40 Like Prometheus
42 Really regret
43 Heart protector
44 Short panties
46 Don Juans
48 Stewed
51 Lagomorphic leapers
54 29-Down competitor
56 Corn ___
59 Outback critter

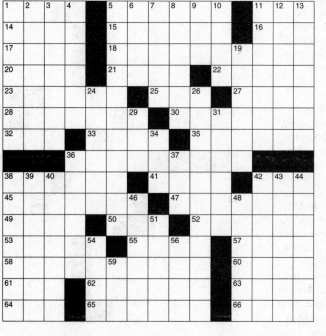

by Edgar R. Fontaine

60

ACROSS

1 Theologian who wrote "Sic et Non"
8 Telephonic timesaver
14 Had to be paid, say
15 Spanish rice ingredient
16 Fictional character with the female slave Morgiana
17 Eternal
18 Milky Way feature
19 "Li'l Abner," once
20 Parenthetically
22 Kind of job
23 Lord who said "Absolute power corrupts absolutely"
24 Social bungler
26 Newcastle Browns, e.g.
27 Looked after
29 They work with stars
31 Ties
33 Try to get
37 Make waves?
42 Where the 2000 World Series ended
43 It might hang over your head
45 Terminate
46 Hair line
47 Kitchen pests
49 Land on the Red Sea
52 Political functions
53 Least likely to be pinned down
54 Like objects dipped in liquid nitrogen
55 Kickers' aids
56 Lift up
57 Brat Pack actress
58 Doctors have them

DOWN

1 Yellow-flowered shrubs
2 What's left
3 Sharjah or Fujairah
4 New Hampshire town south of Hanover
5 Without wavering
6 Sophisticates' opposites
7 Buy and sell
8 Maker of Robusto! sauce
9 Regards
10 Book of Judges villainess
11 They come in shots
12 First name in a Poe poem
13 Lacking support
15 Set equipment
21 Narcotic similar to morphine
25 Big barrel
28 Dim bulbs
30 Tiler's job
32 Works against
33 Looks
34 Rare museum display
35 Point in an ellipse
36 Electrical tower structure
38 One who puts you in your place?
39 "Do I dare believe that?"
40 English actress Winwood
41 They come to terms for terms
44 Attired
48 Feature of some chili
50 Prophesy
51 Annual athletic award

by Patrick Berry

ACROSS

1 Child by marriage
8 Downtown Chicago
15 Percentage listed in an I.R.S. booklet
16 "Good shot!"
17 Woman who's "carrying"
19 Anger, with "up"
20 Summer: Fr.
21 Coin opening
22 Lottery player's exultant cry
23 Obstreperous
26 Wash
27 Put on board, as cargo
28 ___ constrictor
29 Bits of land in la Méditerranée
30 Ogled
31 Yankee Stadium locale, with "the"
33 Role
34 "Vive ___!" (old French cheer)
35 Trail
39 Uncles' mates
40 Shakespearean king
44 On the ocean
45 Schubert's Symphony No. 8 ___ Minor
46 Wheel turner
47 Pie pans
48 Patronizes a library
51 Italian resort on the Adriatic
52 Founded: Abbr.
53 Bill Clinton's relig. affiliation
54 New-___ (devotee of crystals and incense)

55 Traditional end of summer
60 Lenders, often
61 International alliance
62 Summed
63 Appetizer

DOWN

1 Germless
2 What a plane rolls along
3 Go off, as a bomb
4 Dressed up in a fussy way
5 Anatomical pouch
6 Playful aquatic animal
7 "Pretty amazing!"
8 Boom producer, for short
9 "She Done ___ Wrong"
10 Environmental prefix
11 Accidentally reveal
12 "Sexy!"
13 Bogey, in golf
14 Most cheeky
18 Maternity ward arrival
24 Start of a forbiddance
25 Vertical line on a graph
31 British P.M. Tony
32 Get together with old classmates, say
35 Kneecap
36 "Let me repeat . . ."
37 Covered place to sleep

38 Committed, as an act
40 Staples Center player, for short
41 Requiring immediate attention
42 Somewhat firm, as pasta
43 Organize differently, as troops
49 1920's vice president Charles
50 Paid out
56 Wand
57 R & B band ___ Hill
58 Nile viper
59 Greek letter

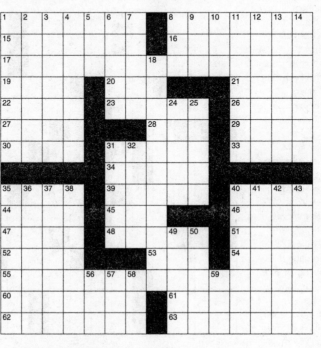

by Michael Shteyman

ACROSS

1 Kind of boom
6 Celeste who won an Oscar for "Gentleman's Agreement"
10 Ticks off
14 "Love Story" author Segal
15 Tribe defeated by the Iroquois
16 Webster who had a way with words
17 Point between Hawaii and Guam
19 Center of a cathedral
20 Mine find
21 Chem. or biol.
22 Narrowed
24 Snapple rival
26 Mary ___ Moore
27 "Oklahoma!" aunt
29 Eye holder
33 Knock out of the sky
36 Pick a card
38 Actress Foch and others
39 "Pumping ___"
40 Divans
42 Civil rights activist Parks
43 Money substitute
45 The end ___ era
46 "Good buddy"
47 Dorothy's home in "The Wizard of Oz"
49 Poker player's declaration
51 Doubting Thomas
53 Spanish dish
57 Silt, e.g.
60 Stick in the water?
61 Crest alternative
62 Jacob's twin
63 Hock shop receipt
66 Ado
67 Gen. Robt. ___
68 "There ___ free lunches"
69 Reporter Clark
70 Some loaves
71 Limb holder?

DOWN

1 Attach, as a patch
2 "___ Ben Jonson" (literary epitaph)
3 Alternatives to Reeboks
4 Rocks at the bar
5 Sculpt
6 Prefix with port or pad
7 ___ pro nobis
8 Like a dryer trap
9 Some awards
10 Group of confidants
11 Surf's sound
12 Gutter location
13 Place for a mower
18 Heats just short of boiling
23 Unskilled laborer
25 Place for sets and lets
26 Word that can precede the last word of 17- and 63-Across and 10- and 25-Down
28 Suffix with switch
30 Door opener
31 Facilitate
32 Russian leader before 1917
33 Tiddlywink, e.g.
34 Shamu, for one
35 Slightly tattered
37 Female W.W. II grp.
41 Attack verbally
44 Settles up
48 Concealed shooter
50 Rodeo rope
52 "Boot" in the Mediterranean
54 Los Angeles player
55 Property claims
56 Response to "Are not!"
57 Office necessity
58 Villa d'___
59 What an analgesic stops
60 Addition column
64 Minute
65 ___-Magnon

by Sarah Keller

ACROSS

1 Son of Judah
5 "Ba-da-___!"
9 Clearly
14 Baseball's Hideo ___
15 Words with a nod
16 Like Cro-Magnon man, to us
17 Got down
18 Keaton's "Mr. Mom" co-star
19 Struck from the Bible?
20 Narcissist's breakup line?
23 Fix, as old shoes
24 San Francisco's ___ Hill
25 Radio host's breakup line?
32 Audiophile's shelfful
35 One way to go to a party
36 "I understand, sir!"
37 Cupid's counterpart
39 Tease
41 First name in mystery
42 Easy to prepare, say
45 Accurse
48 Get-up-and-go
49 Astronaut's breakup line?
52 1988 Meg Ryan film
53 Cotton Bowl city
57 Farmer's breakup line?
62 Breakfast sizzler
63 Korea's Syngman ___
64 Retin-A treats it
65 Rod-shaped germ
66 Till slot
67 John Astin's actor son
68 They're verboten
69 Thai restaurant cookware
70 Rice-shaped pasta

DOWN

1 Sign in a station
2 Nick of "The Deep"
3 Out of place
4 "Later!"
5 Center of a circus
6 "Because ___ so!"
7 Fictional Wolfe
8 "-ing" word
9 Gaffer's aide
10 Traditional Thanksgiving dish
11 Word on a gift tag
12 Old, to Oskar
13 White alternative
21 Arena yells
22 Smidgen
26 Pencil holder
27 "Zounds!"
28 Ball holder
29 Org. for boomers, now
30 Singer Lovett
31 Stay fresh
32 Filmmaker Riefenstahl
33 Figurehead's place
34 Crash site?
38 Light source
40 Old Navy's parent, with "The"
43 France's patron
44 It might make you short of breath
46 March ___ (47-Down tourney)
47 School sports org.
50 Peter of Peter, Paul and Mary
51 Rio Grande city
54 Football factory worker
55 Ball's partner
56 Pool member of old
57 Baylor's city
58 B-school subj.
59 Electrical unit
60 "This can't be!"
61 Pay period
62 Rose's home

by Steve Jones

ACROSS

1 Smudge
5 Quiet times
10 Hole maker
14 Call's companion
15 One in search of a tin can
16 Parrot
17 Hesitation by actor William?
19 Fats Waller's "___ I'll Be Tired of You"
20 Peeved
21 Rustling sound
23 Peanut Butter Lovers Mo.
24 River of Hesse
26 Abed
28 Garden figure
30 Don't just stand there
33 Piz Bernina, e.g.
34 Suffix with modern
36 Reason for a citation: Abbr.
37 A large order
38 Contract term for a 1930's heavyweight champ?
41 1974 Gould/ Sutherland spoof
43 Farm cry
44 Select, with "for"
45 Neither's partner
46 Handle clumsily
48 Crocheted item
52 Bit of nostalgia
54 Leaves home?
56 Key opener?
57 Vivacity
60 Straddling
62 Org. with eligibility rules
63 Actor Russell's Oscar win?
65 Is beneficial

66 Trade fair-goer
67 Greatness
68 Travel plans: Abbr.
69 ___ Yello (soft drink)
70 Went down

DOWN

1 "The Thrill Is Gone" hitmaker, 1970
2 Use for support
3 Book specification
4 Ducats: Abbr.
5 One of a team of eight
6 Lessener
7 Cardinals great ___ Brock
8 It may be high in church
9 Do a slow boil
10 "Ditto"

11 Biography of a noted newspaper publisher?
12 Comic book hero since 1962
13 Babydoll
18 Cause for a blessing
22 Ft. Erie's home
25 Revolutionary War soldier
27 Later afterthought: Abbr.
29 G.I.'s not accounted for
31 Leather sticker
32 "Later!"
35 First name in humor
37 Job preceder: Abbr.
38 Famed admiral's concurrence?

39 Spread
40 Tournament shockers
41 ___-Jet (winter vehicle)
42 Skunk
46 Apiece
47 Mason's aid
49 Attorney's filing
50 Introspective query
51 Stole
53 Bridge declaration
55 Summer time in Buenos Aires
58 Long-range weapon, for short
59 Align
61 Switch positions
62 Popular news source, briefly
64 Olive ___

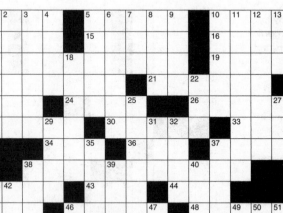

by Peter Abide

65

ACROSS

1 "Ta-ta!"
6 Painting
12 Angular measurement
14 Staged event
15 N.B.A. All-Star Allen
17 World Series-winning manager, 1981 and 1988
18 Has an early lead
20 Nester
21 Discombobulated
22 1970's TV character whose real first name was Arthur, with "the"
23 Literary orphan adopted by the Dursleys
24 Assemblies
25 London borough with Wimbledon Stadium
26 "Speed" star
27 Give heed
28 Sassy girls
29 Activist?
30 2004 Olympic track gold medalist ___ Gatlin
31 Warmth
32 Wisconsin college or its city
33 Fed
34 Was on easy street
37 Strauss's "___ und Verklärung"
38 Serving as a diplomat below the rank of ambassador
40 Where to find a pig, maybe
42 Capital of the Solomon Islands
43 Like things?
44 Suddenly quits running
45 Closed with a lock
46 Beginning

DOWN

1 It may be blue, brown or green
2 Expert
3 Emerson's "___ Beauty"
4 I
5 Efficient employee
6 Do together
7 "As I Lay Dying" father
8 E-7, e.g.: Abbr.
9 Paul who directed "Basic Instinct"
10 Champagne department
11 Parts of numbers
13 Pitching feat
14 St. ___ River, separating Michigan from Ontario
16 Shipping weight
19 Fen-___ (former diet drug combo)
22 In modern lingo, a vegetarian who occasionally eats meat
24 In art, an underlying image that's been painted over
25 Actress who played the Bond girl Octopussy
26 Trattoria side dishes
27 Daughter of Ares
28 Stubborn
29 Spiteful
30 Knight at the movies
32 Spoilers
34 Raised
35 Parts of some meters
36 Country singer Steve
38 Unwelcome C.I.A. discovery
39 Go on
41 Doozy

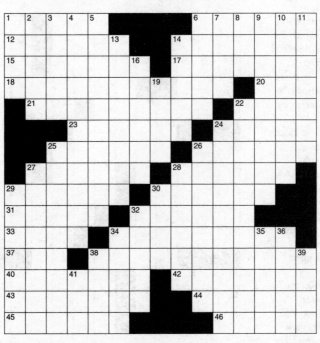

by Brendan Emmett Quigley

ACROSS

1 Ill-fated emperor of 1502–20
10 Marine tank
15 "I'm waiting"
16 Instrument Paul McCartney played on Ringo Starr's "You're Sixteen"
17 Getting down
18 Permanently
19 The last thing a Yale cheerleader wants
20 Scruffy
22 Southeast-most county of Ireland, or its seat
25 Tycoons' holdings
29 Backslider?
31 California city NW of Bakersfield
32 Kiwis
36 English county from which the Pilgrims set sail in 1620
37 Take up, perhaps
38 Spaniard's "that"
39 First secretary of H.E.W., 1953, ___ Culp Hobby
40 Santa ___
41 Messiah
43 Buffalo's AAA baseball team
45 Face saver
46 Cold start
48 Astronomical distances
52 Blank page
54 Filch
55 Holy Roman emperor crowned 962
58 Clayey rock once common in building

61 Attach, in a way
62 Passing legislation?
63 Mexican War general known as Old Fuss and Feathers
64 Checks

DOWN

1 Large bird with a loud scream
2 See 57-Down
3 Half of a 1997 telecom merger
4 Successful field results, for short
5 Lac contents
6 The chemistry of fermentation
7 Hard to research

8 Figure in Umberto Eco's "The Name of the Rose"
9 "Shucks!"
10 Not chosen
11 Structural supports
12 Certain gun
13 French compliment
14 Fine, slangily
21 Roman square?
23 Swift
24 1966 James Bond spoof
26 Obvious lunatic
27 Short message via AOL, say
28 Bat signals?
30 Button for pins
32 Luxor locals
33 Confine

34 2003 Nick Lachey hit "___ Swear"
35 Arias
42 Like Elgar's Symphony No.1
44 Sneaking
47 Baseball Hall-of-Famer Flick
49 Gastrointestinal danger
50 Big name in late-night TV
51 Throws off
53 Let up
55 Old spy grp.
56 Shamus
57 With 2-Down, certain mismatch
59 Orch. part
60 Some like it hot

by Byron Walden

ACROSS

1 Raindrop sound
5 Sgt., e.g.
8 Present for a teacher
13 Kelly of morning TV
14 Marlboro alternative
15 Shine
16 Son of Isaac
17 Metal that Superman can't see through
18 On again, as a candle
19 Fashionable London locale
21 Ardor
22 Big containers
23 Filmmaker Spike
24 GM sports car
27 Whitewater part of a stream
30 Fireplace accessory
32 UK record label
33 Cast member
36 Hits head-on
37 Get help of a sort on "Who Wants to Be a Millionaire"
41 Wriggling fishes
42 Place
43 Tit for ___
44 Teems
47 Zoo denizens
49 Something "on the books"
50 Motorists' grp.
51 Skier's transport
52 Quick job for a barber
54 Sweater
58 To no ___ (purposelessly)
60 Classic artist's subject
61 Sandwich spread, for short

62 Oscar who wrote "The Picture of Dorian Gray"
63 Popular shirt label
64 Certain stock index
65 Los Angeles cager
66 Craggy hill
67 Agile

DOWN

1 Make ready, for short
2 Elvis's daughter ___ Marie
3 Milky gem
4 1960's–70's pontiff
5 December songs
6 Fuel from a mine
7 Bygone
8 Consented
9 Bit of begging
10 Educational assistance since 1972
11 China's Chou En-___
12 Expert in resuscitation, in brief
14 Coffee gathering
20 Angry with
21 ___ state (blissful self-awareness)
23 Lash of old westerns
25 Frisky feline
26 Beginnings
27 Statute removal
28 Itsy-bitsy creature
29 Bedtime gab
31 Anger
34 Actress Allen of "Enough"
35 Cheerios grain

38 Baton Rouge sch.
39 Tried a little of this, a little of that
40 Rarely-met goal
45 Hammer user
46 Hoover ___
48 Scents
51 Henry VIII's family name
53 Travel on horseback
54 Mario who wrote "The Godfather"
55 Seductress
56 Witness
57 Classic theater name
58 Leatherworker's tool
59 By way of
60 Annual hoops contest, for short

by Jay Giess

ACROSS

1 Dispensable candy
4 On pins and needles
8 Meeting
14 "The Name of the Rose" writer
15 Chaucer offering
16 1966 Mary Martin musical
17 Dog with an upturned tail
19 Big-time brat
20 Sluggin' Sammy
21 Glasgow gal
23 Master's worker
24 Gambler's marker
26 Choice word
29 Give one's word
35 Beantown team, briefly
36 Press release?
37 Santa ___, Calif.
38 Holder of two tablets
39 Mingling with
42 Camera type, briefly
43 Taoism founder Lao-___
44 Horror film staple
45 Site of a racing win or a tie
47 Traditional elocution exercise
51 Beheaded Boleyn
52 Den denizen
53 Injure seriously
56 Limp watch painter
58 Sci-fi sightings
62 Take stock of
65 Intellectual
67 Fire escape, e.g.
68 Turkish honorific
69 Clean air grp.
70 Be obsequious
71 One of the "Little Women"
72 Letters for a psychic

DOWN

1 They're above the abs
2 It might be off the wall
3 Animal keepers
4 And so on: Abbr.
5 Veronica Lake film "The Blue ___"
6 What a poor winner does
7 They have boughs for bows
8 Peach part
9 Words from Wordsworth
10 Go downhill
11 Put a traveling mike on
12 Reason for nose-pinching
13 Klingon on the Enterprise
18 Odd fellow
22 Baseball commissioner Bud
25 Honeycomb shape
27 Periscope part
28 "The Bartered Bride" composer
29 Trunk with a chest
30 Out of kilter
31 Dog tag datum
32 Explorer ___ da Gama
33 Not at full power
34 Job for a dermatologist
35 Ordeal for Rover, perhaps
40 Like a trim lawn
41 Globular
46 Second-stringer
48 "Anything you want"
49 Make beholden
50 Scale reading
53 Halloween accessory
54 Concerning
55 Middle of Caesar's boast
57 "Moby-Dick" captain
59 Unbind
60 "My bad!"
61 Give and take
63 Sign of a sellout
64 Opposite NNE
66 "I told you so!"

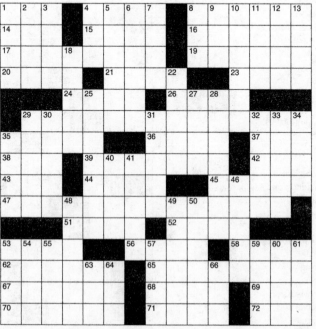

by Nancy Salomon and Harvey Estes

ACROSS

1 Potato chip, to a Brit
6 Willy Wonka's creator
10 Little ones
14 Year-end temp
15 Plane measure
16 City south of Moscow
17 A pronoun has one
19 Bit of cunning
20 "The Omega Man" star, 1971
21 New arrival, of sorts
23 Maureen Dowd piece
25 "Get a grip!"
27 Straw source
28 60's trip cause
29 Teutonic surname starter
30 Chest item
31 Astronomical discovery of 1930
33 Somber song
35 "Ruthless People" star
39 Tony winner Swoosie
40 African antelope
43 Rover's warning
46 Former U.S. mil. acronym
47 Big poker player's wager
49 Clinch
50 Engage in woolgathering?
53 Old TV problem
54 Military surprise
55 No longer in effect
57 Box lightly
58 Battle cry
62 Narcissist's love
63 Came down
64 Knock senseless
65 Poker player's calculation
66 Famous rhymer of Bronx with "thonx"
67 Aggressive sort

DOWN

1 Lee's org.
2 Sought a seat
3 Taking a bath
4 Tilter's mount
5 Donation-soliciting grps.
6 Set into a groove
7 Where the action is
8 Farm layer
9 Up-to-the-minute news
10 Namely
11 Properly
12 Texas border city
13 Hazardous for driving, maybe
18 J.F.K. postings
22 Was sociable, in a way
23 Alley ___
24 Bud
26 Mid first-century year
28 "Odyssey" morsels
32 Shatner sci-fi drug
33 Noncombat area, for short
34 Electric ___
36 "Circular file"
37 Use acid
38 Start of a deluge
41 One above a specialist: Abbr.
42 It may become hoarfrost
43 Former Connecticut governor Ella
44 Wheelchair-accessible
45 Like Playboy cartoons
47 The haves have it
48 Date with an M.D.
51 Browses, today
52 Perry of fashion
53 Serta rival
56 Wishy-washy
59 Taking after
60 Cohort of Curly
61 Sp. lady

by Alan Arbesfeld

ACROSS

1 ___ Israel
5 Pink-slip
9 Title girl of a 1986 #1 Starship hit
13 Indy winner Luyendyk
14 Arthur of the court
15 Blemished, in a way
16 Laughing 1970's singer?
18 Parson's home
19 Weather map line
20 Total
22 Man in a garden
24 Dominant
25 Honey bunch?
28 Tot's wheels
31 Kung Fu-___ (alternative name for Confucius)
34 Copacetic
35 Large fishing nets
36 Thieves' take
37 "Dear" one
38 Laughing comment when something's all over?
39 Walletful
40 Confronted
41 Crabbed
42 Overnight dance party
43 Workplace watchdog, for short
44 Actor Joe of "Hill Street Blues"
45 Kind of cake
46 Box office take
48 Boat with an open hold
50 Continental ways?

54 Up next
58 Opposite of wild
59 Laughing fictional detective?
61 Ivy Leaguer's home
62 Like a line, briefly
63 "Such a pity . . ."
64 A few
65 Not as much
66 Run

DOWN

1 Mideast believer
2 Slips
3 Beginner: Var.
4 Alluring greeting
5 Oasis place
6 Nile biter
7 Tony
8 Bingo relative
9 Skull cap?
10 Laughing literary wife?
11 What the defense may do
12 "Zip-___-Doo-Dah"
15 Most plentiful
17 Rotters
21 Get while the getting's good
23 In myth, home of the Cyclops
25 ___ Girl
26 Steinbeck characters
27 Laughing choreographer?
29 Up
30 Emcees' lines
32 Debonair
33 One sought for advice
35 Make a point, perhaps

38 Burrito alternative
42 Short end of the stick
45 Actress Anderson
47 Novelist Walker
49 Causes of coughs
50 Sales tag notation
51 Stick ___
52 Forester's concern: Abbr.
53 1953 Oscar-nominated film based on a novel by Jack Schaefer
55 Lover of Narcissus
56 Boxing sobriquet
57 Trouser part
60 Latin thing

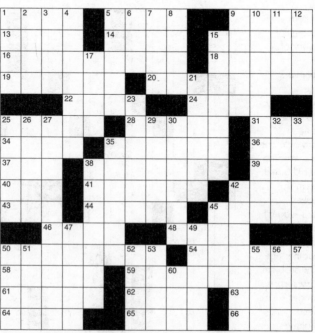

by Paula Gamache

ACROSS
1 Place not much heard from
9 Mr. on "Mission: Impossible"
15 How spokes go
16 "Hey, hey, hey!"
17 2004 political exile
18 "Friends" actress
19 Rejoices (in)
20 Is divisive
21 What England's George VI lacked
22 One pulling strings?
23 Exotic land, in verse
25 Whence Ahab's story
26 Its first song was "Video Killed the Radio Star"
29 Cargo carrier
30 Pouter's riposte
32 Speaking one's mind?
34 Familiar redhead since 1918
35 "Empedocles on ___" (Matthew Arnold poem)
36 Blood letters
37 Lots
38 Snorkelers' wear
39 Carried
40 Hunky-dory
41 Melodic musical passages
44 Brendan Behan's "___ Boy"
47 Rancho ___ (fossil site)
48 Main way to a 49-Across, maybe
49 Popular vacation spot
50 Tells
51 High points
52 Neon or helium

DOWN
1 Bring unwillingly
2 ___ of Avon
3 Western "so long"
4 Stripping
5 Luxuriously smooth
6 Layers
7 Futuramic of the late 40's and early 50's
8 Ship rope or chain
9 Mocking, with "at"
10 Be a homebody?
11 Like Esau vis-à-vis Jacob
12 ___ de Triomphe
13 Bit of intrigue
14 They may be pulled in two directions
20 Woes for toes
22 Draw
23 Ad ___ per aspera (Kansas' motto)
24 Doctor's order
25 Mau Maus, e.g.
26 Chiang Ch'ing's mate
27 Big case
28 Sacred Hindu text
30 Byways
31 Takes all the money from
33 Camper's supply
38 Kaleidoscope part
39 Natural cleanser
40 Might
41 Amman's Queen ___ International Airport
42 File
43 Suffix with discern
44 "Très ___!"
45 The U.N.'s Kofi ___ Annan
46 Lacking
48 Actress Meyers

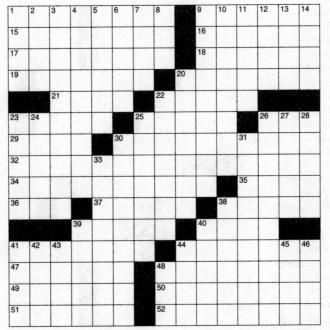

by Manny Nosowsky

ACROSS

1 Treat for tired dogs?
8 Source of a large, colorful lingo
15 Better
16 1983 Randy Newman song with the lyric "Looks like another perfect day"
17 Lazybones
18 Select
19 Store need: Abbr.
20 $60 property in Monopoly
22 Unleashes (upon)
23 Take off
25 Wit who recorded the classic 1960 comedy album "At the Hungry I"
26 Film equipment, for short
27 Children's author Eleanor
29 Stag
31 Prompter's whisper
32 Specialty retailer since 1969
34 Establish as a goal
36 Antique store section
38 Like some police
41 Bright wrap
45 Airplane part
46 "___ way, please"
48 Beaujolais grape
49 Health org.
50 They're spotted in ponds
52 Modern conference beginning
53 Soprano Jenny
55 Is out

57 "Snuffy Smith" parent
58 Finished
60 Starting guide
62 Brahms work that includes "Behold All Flesh"
63 It's blue
64 Having the will?
65 Villain, at times

DOWN

1 Scene of a lot of shooting
2 "Man alive!"
3 Be in charge of
4 Musical syllable
5 Ex-Sen. Charles
6 Iris locales
7 Uproar
8 Basis on which many suits are pressed

9 Legislative group
10 Moonshine
11 Birds, in Latin
12 Perennial government concern
13 Philippine language
14 Crew members
21 "Oh, well"
24 Popular music genre
28 Stash (away)
30 Times
31 Ogle
33 Split
35 Lake of rock's Emerson, Lake & Palmer
37 It's said before God
38 Having pricked ears

39 Name on a ticket
40 Manners
42 Autobiographical subtitle
43 Actor in both "Shane," 1953, and "City Slickers," 1991
44 Spectacles
47 Cordwood units
51 Give the cold shoulder
54 Old Test. book
55 Mincemeat ingredient
56 Thorny Eurasian shrub
59 Opposite of noche
61 Quebec's Festival d'___

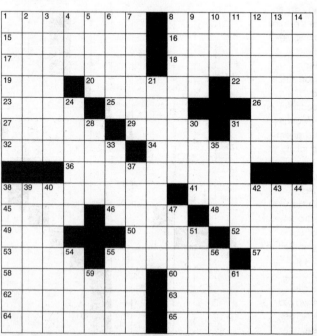

by Bob Peoples

73

ACROSS

1 Go to sea
5 Feet above sea level: Abbr.
9 Boston's airport
14 Stubborn animal
15 Ear part
16 Ex-Mrs. Trump
17 Fitzgerald who sang "I'm Making Believe"
18 University V.I.P.
19 Car parker
20 Decreed
23 ___ foil
24 Before, in verse
25 Fleming of 007 fame
26 Bad mark
28 Discontinued
29 Lacking muscle
33 Writer Welty
35 Throng
36 Document of legal representation
40 Liqueur flavoring
41 Armadas
42 Nary a soul
43 Injection units, for short
44 Relaxed
48 Tree swinger
49 Joanne of "Sylvia," 1965
50 1959 hit song about "a man named Charlie"
51 Children's game
56 Easy gallops
57 Bad place to drop a heavy box
58 Landed (on)
59 Florida city
60 Advantage
61 Ready for picking
62 Like sea air
63 Flagmaker Betsy
64 1930's boxer Max

DOWN

1 Refines, as metal
2 How some café is served
3 "Fighting" Big Ten team
4 Starring role
5 Fabled New World city
6 "Camelot" composer
7 Israel's Abba
8 Open the windows in
9 Jazz up
10 Running track
11 Festive party
12 Again
13 ___ King Cole
21 Shy
22 "This ___ better be good!"
27 Honkers
28 Rigorous exams
29 On the downslide
30 Sea eagle
31 Lemon or lime drink
32 C minor, for one
34 Unbalanced
35 Spa feature
36 Criticize, as a movie
37 Plastic ___ Band
38 Victory
39 Fragrant flowers
43 Overseer of co. books
45 Earhart who disappeared over the Pacific
46 Skunk feature
47 It immediately follows Passiontide
48 Examine, as ore
49 Bottom of the barrel
51 ___-Cola
52 Iridescent stone
53 Skin
54 One slow on the uptake
55 Cutting remark
56 The "L" of L.A.

by A. J. Santora

ACROSS

1 Unconsciousness
5 Govt. security
10 Tell all
14 Eve's mate
15 North of talk radio
16 Leave in the dust
17 Player of Ginger
19 A few chips in the pot, maybe
20 Kind of scene in a movie
21 Other, to Ortega
22 Inspirations
23 Player of the title role in 37-Across
26 [Woe is me!]
30 Social historian Jacob
31 Charles Lamb, pseudonymously
32 Desist
34 Ewe's cry
37 Classic sitcom that debuted on 9/26/1964
41 ___ sauce
42 Blue-haired lady of TV cartoons
43 Ye ___ Shoppe
44 7-Eleven, e.g.
45 Adorable "bears"
47 Player of Thurston Howell III
50 Half-man/half-goat creatures
52 ___-majesté
53 Org. that helps with motel discounts
56 Remark while putting chips in the pot
57 Player of the Skipper
60 Mexican fast food
61 Mob
62 "I smell ___!"

63 Slow-boil
64 Got up
65 Hunky-___

DOWN

1 See 3-Down
2 "Garfield" dog
3 With 1-Down, tailless pets
4 Doctor's org.
5 Overly
6 Squib on a book jacket
7 Ancient Greek class reading
8 Fleur-de-___
9 Name that's a homophone of 8-Down
10 Shivs
11 Society avoider
12 Nick and Nora's pooch

13 Spelling contests
18 Gray wolf
22 Harvard, Yale, Princeton, etc., for short
24 Rub out
25 Not yet final, at law
26 Importunes
27 Mixture
28 Greasy
29 Actor Linden or Holbrook
32 Magna ___
33 Essay writer's class: Abbr.
34 Shiny on top?
35 "Three Men ___ Baby"
36 Summer drinks
38 Some prayer leaders
39 Dress

40 Actor Chaney
44 Boat on 37-Across
45 Shoved
46 Lost
47 Result of squeezing, maybe
48 Mild cigar
49 Japanese form of fencing
50 Partner of starts
51 Latin 101 verb
53 Prefix with nautical
54 Slightly open
55 Creative
57 Responses to a masseur
58 Home stretch?
59 Irish fellow

by Andrea Carla Michaels

ACROSS

1 Code word for "A"
5 Jostle
10 Mockery
14 Blackens
15 Model Gabrielle
16 "Unimaginable as ___ in Heav'n": Milton
17 Understood
18 Popular 80's–90's TV sitcom
20 "Let's Make ___"
22 Elton John, e.g.
23 Clarinetist Shaw
24 ___ the world
26 A different approach
28 Slalom course move
29 William who has a state named after him
31 Slippery sort
32 Lulu
34 Shakes up
36 In case that's true
40 Olin of "Hollywood Homicide," 2003
41 Charge
42 "___ and Lovers" (D. H. Lawrence book)
43 Italian wine-growing region
44 1973 #1 Rolling Stones hit
45 Chisel or gouge
46 Big maker of A.T.M.'s
48 Yes ___
50 Cube root of eight
51 Monkey business
55 Blown snow
57 Midwest home of ConAgra
58 Corp. money head
60 Holy ___
62 Tumbler
65 Halo
66 Newsman Sevareid
67 Sauce with jalapeño
68 Any of the Phillies, e.g.
69 Winter Olympics venue
70 Oversized volume
71 "___ Heartache" (Bonnie Tyler hit)

DOWN

1 Aleutian island
2 Hidden dangers
3 Player without a contract
4 Dam on the Nile
5 Suffix with east
6 Island rings
7 September equinox, and a hint to the starts of 18- & 62-Across and 2-, 3-, 10-, 33-, 37- & 38-Down
8 Yellow shade
9 Dewy
10 Place for a select group
11 High-class, as a restaurant
12 Take ___ (travel)
13 Allots, with "out"
19 Lawyer's undertaking
21 Cut (off)
25 Maserati competitor
27 London theater district
28 "La Débâcle" novelist
30 Verb preceder
33 Consolation of a sort
35 Den
37 Court infraction
38 Winter driving aid
39 See 64-Down
47 Blacken
49 Assn.
51 Lawn Boy product
52 Japanese porcelain
53 Audited, with "on"
54 Conspicuous success
56 Shiraz native
59 Greek peak
61 Boris Pasternak heroine
63 Fed. construction overseer
64 Airline to 39-Down

by David J. Kahn

42

You'll Never Be Clueless.

The New York Times Crossword Society

Join now and receive six classic Times puzzles every month, selected from the best of Sunday crosswords and printed on high-quality oversized paper — easy to write on and take with you.

One-year membership
$44.95 – U.S.
$54.95 – Canada and Mexico
$69.95 – overseas
Call 1-888-7ACROSS
(1-888-722-7677)
Payment by American Express,
MasterCard or Visa

The New York Times
CROSSWORD SOCIETY

1

<pre>
G R I D   D A T E   S T A L E
A E R O   O M A R   T I M E X
B L O C   R A V I   R E E V E
S Y N T H E T I C F A B R I C
      R A M   O N A
A R T I F I C I A L G R A S S
M O U N T   A N N I E   L E E
A R T E   O P T I C   M E N D
T E T   B U R R O   L O U S E
I M I T A T I O N B U T T E R
      A R R   A S H
C O U N T E R F E I T B I L L
H O R D E   E A R L   A L O E
U N S E R   E R I E   L I N T
M A A M S   L E N D   L A G S
</pre>

2

<pre>
A T B A T   G O L F S   I C E
M O O L A   A W E E K   S O D
B R A I N F R E E Z E   O L D
E S T   G I R D S   T O S A Y
R O S E L L E   A C D C
      M E L T E D C H E E S E
W H A M S   A I R Y   L I D
R O B E   M A S S E   D E L I
A U S   S A L E   A I S L E
P R E T T Y P L E A S E
    N O R A   S C H M E A R
G O T T A   T O P I C   L S U
A P E   F L O R I D A K E Y S
Z E E   E A G L E   N O N E T
E L S   S T A Y S   S P A T S
</pre>

3

<pre>
M S N B C   R E I D   E W A N
U H A U L   E D N A   R A T E
C A N Y O U H E A R M E N O W
H M O   S P A N S   I N E P T
      A E O N   E N T O
T E S T I N G O N E T W O
A V I A N   I S A Y   R N A
M E N D   J A N E T   Z I O N
E R A   S O C K   B O N G O
      I S T H I S T H I N G O N
      T E N D   W A G E
C H A I N   T A I L S   A F T
H E L L O H E L L O H E L L O
A R A L   A S T I   O N E A M
D O N S   S T A T   T E X T S
</pre>

4

<pre>
A T E U P   M O N A   T A M P
B A S S O   O B I S   O G E E
C L A S S   L I M B   R E N T
S K I R T E D T H E I S S U E
      I R E   S R O
    B E L T E D O U T A S O N G
N O V A S   C M O N   D Y E
O W E D   S E E P S   C O M A
T I N   G I L A   P U R E R
V E S T E D I N T E R E S T
      O N E   U T E
S O C K E D I N T H E N O S E
A X L E   I S E E   M A U L S
F E I N   S L O E   P T R A P
E N O S   H E N S   T E S T Y
</pre>

5

<pre>
T R O T T E R   M A C H E T E
R I V I E R A   E S S A Y E R
I C E L A N D   S L A V I N G
C E R T   S I A M   E N T O
K A L   S T A G E F R I G H T
K R O N E   T U R R E T
N O R E A S O N   E L M I R A
E N D O W E R   I D E A M E N
E I S N E R   S T A N D P A T
    L E V I E S   T E R S E
I N C I D E N T A L S   E S A
D O U G   L A M A   S C U T
T O S H I B A   E N S N A R E
A S H T R A Y   S C O O T E R
G E Y S E R S   S E A B E D S
</pre>

6

S	C	A	M	S		G	L	A	D		C	O	M	A
P	U	R	E	E		R	O	B	E		A	U	L	D
I	T	I	N	A		O	N	L	Y	C	H	I	L	D
K	I	T	T	R	E	D	G	E		R	O	S	E	S
E	T	H	I	O	P	I	A		L	O	O			
	M	O	V	I	N	G	P	I	C	T	U	R	E	
T	H	E	N	E	T		O	A	K		S	N	I	T
R	O	T		R	H	O		D	E	F		A	G	A
E	M	I	T		E	S	P		W	O	M	B	A	T
S	E	C	R	E	T	A	D	M	I	R	E	R		
		A	L	S		J	U	S	T	M	I	S	S	
C	L	A	I	M		C	A	T	E	R	E	D	T	O
C	Y	C	L	O	R	A	M	A		E	N	G	E	L
E	R	T	E		E	V	E	N		S	T	E	N	T
D	E	E	R		F	E	S	T		S	O	D	O	I

7

W	A	V	E		F	A	R	M		M	A	R	K	S
A	U	E	R		A	R	E	A		I	N	A	L	L
X	X	X	R	A	T	I	N	G		R	A	D	I	O
			A	R	C		E	N	G	A	G	I	N	G
S	C	O	T	I	A		W	A	R	C	R	I	E	S
P	A	P	I	S	T	S			I	L	A			
O	N	I	C	E		A	A	A	M	E	M	B	E	R
R	A	N			B	B	B				R	N	A	
E	L	E	V	E	N	E	E	E		A	M	A	S	S
			A	X	E			T	A	P	E	S	U	P
S	T	E	N	C	I	L	S		R	I	N	S	E	S
P	E	N	D	U	L	U	M		A	N	D			
A	N	D	Y	S		G	E	O	R	G	E	I	I	I
S	T	O	K	E		E	L	L	A		R	O	A	N
M	O	R	E	S		S	T	E	T		S	U	N	K

8

A	S	F	A	R		L	S	A	T	S		F	I	G
L	A	R	G	O		E	P	C	O	T		I	R	A
K	I	E	R	K	E	G	A	A	R	D		N	O	R
A	N	S	E		T	A	R	D	E		D	E	N	Y
	T	H	E	A	C	T			I	S	N	T		
		S	C	H	O	P	E	N	H	A	U	E	R	
S	M	O	T	E			R	O	T	E		N	C	O
H	A	L	O		D	R	A	N	O		R	E	O	S
A	M	Y		F	I	N	N		S	A	D	L	Y	
H	A	M	M	A	R	S	K	J	O	L	D			
	P	E	N	T			E	R	R	A	T	A		
T	W	I	N		P	L	A	T	S		R	A	R	E
E	R	A		M	O	U	S	S	O	R	G	S	K	Y
R	A	D		G	O	A	P	E		O	U	T	I	E
M	P	S		T	R	U	S	T		O	N	E	N	D

9

M	E	N	S	A		A	C	A	D		D	I	S	C
P	A	N	T	S		L	O	G	E		O	B	O	E
S	T	E	E	P		E	L	I	A		D	I	B	S
		W	I	N	K	A	N	D	R	O	S	E	S	
A	H	A		R	U	E		E	A	S	E	I	N	
P	A	R	K	I	N	G	F	I	N	K		S	T	A
B	R	I	A	N			L	O	D	E	S			
S	P	A	M		C	L	A	N	S		A	D	A	M
		A	S	H	E	N			P	R	I	C	E	
S	P	A		L	I	N	K	O	F	S	I	G	H	T
A	R	T	F	U	L		S	R	A		S	E	E	
M	A	K	E	M	I	N	E	M	I	N	K			
I	N	I	T		D	E	V	O		D	I	N	G	Y
A	C	N	E		O	M	E	N		Q	T	I	P	S
M	E	S	S		G	O	L	D		S	E	P	A	L

10

A	S	I	F		S	W	E	E	P		A	T	O	Z
L	A	N	A		T	H	R	E	E		L	O	N	I
M	A	R	L		O	I	L	E	R		T	M	E	N
A	B	I	C	Y	C	L	E		I	A	M	B	I	C
	O	A	K	S			I	O	W	A				
	C	A	N	T	S	T	A	N	D	O	N	I	T	S
B	A	R	R			T	O	I	L		S	E	A	
O	R	G	Y		N	S	Y	N	C		L	I	E	N
N	E	O		T	I	T	O			A	T	M	S	
O	W	N	B	E	C	A	U	S	E	I	T	I	S	
	I	C	K	Y		A	C	T	V					
S	T	J	O	H	N		T	W	O	T	I	R	E	D
M	O	E	N		A	F	O	F	L		A	I	D	E
U	G	L	I		M	A	R	I	E		N	O	N	E
T	A	L	C		E	D	I	T	S		S	T	A	R

11

```
Q U E E R E Y E   M A R C E L
U P I N A R M S   A P E R C U
A N N E R I C E   D O T E L L
      M I C A   O E D I P A L
C A P I T A   H U P   T E T
H A L E Y   M I T R A L
I R A S   M I S S O R E G O N
L O N   R U N S O U T   U N E
I N T H E F I E L D   G R O W
    U N F O L D   M O U N T
  F A R   I N F   R A I S E S
P O L L E N S   T E N N
E N L I S T   W I N D G U S T
A D O N A I   A V E M A R I A
R A Y G U N   D O E S T I M E
```

12

```
S P O R T S B R A   E L I H U
W I N E T H I E F   T E N O N
O P E N O R D E R   S I L L S
R E B   P E E N   B E S I D E
E D Y S   D R A M A Q U E E N
T O O L E   S C A B   R U N T
O W N E R S   T R I B E
  N E E D E D   V E R S E S
    P E P U P   S A U N A S
C C V I   I N I T   T I T L E
R A I N M A K E R S   T I E S
O M E G A S   R O A R   C S T
W E N C H   D R I V E T I M E
D I N A R   P O K E F U N A T
S N A R E   S T A R S I G N S
```

13

```
T A S T E   S W A M P   T I L
A N T E S   P A N E L   O N E
B Y Y E S T E R D A Y   U T E
    E R A S   W A T E R
S P O O N E R   P R O U D L Y
H E N L E Y   C H O O S E
R A T E S   R O A L D   S U N
E C H O   P U R S E   T U N E
W E E   M E L E E   B R I D E
  D O O L E Y   L O O T E D
A M O U N T S   F I N D E R S
B O U T S   A L O E
O R B   T H I S I N S T A N T
M E L   E E R I E   U R I A H
B Y E   R E E F S   P A R T Y
```

14

```
B R A S S   S T E N O   S A P
E A T U P   P I N E A P P L E
A R O M A   E N T E R T A I N
R E P O R T C A R D   E R A S
        S I S S Y   P R E S
S T A M E N     S A O
L O V E   C O R K E R   P E W
A A A A A A A A A A A A A A A A A A A A
M T S   I N T E N T   L I V Y
    D R S     T R A D E S
  A L E S   S C A L A
F D I C   P E R F E C T G P A
A L M A M A T E R   E R R O L
T E A F O R T W O   R E A D E
S R S   D R E S S   S E N S E
```

15

```
B O S H   B A S R A   S A D A
A R C O   E M A I L   U X O R
L I R R   T U R T L E N E C K
L O U N G E L I Z A R D
A L F   O L E S   M R M O M
D E F R O S T   A L I E N E E
E S S E   S P O N S O R S
  S N A K E E Y E S
M E C H A N I C   E S M E
D E P O N E D   B R I S T O L
S N O U T   A E O N   R O E
  L E A P F R O G G I N G
T O A D S T O O L S   A P I A
A N N E   M E R I T   P E E N
G E A R   O M E N S   E R S T
```

16

```
R O B T ■ P A L E ■ U P F O R
U T A H ■ E N I D ■ H U R O N
T O T E ■ T U T U ■ A L O H A
H O T[DOG]W I T H[CAT]S U P ■
A L L S E T ■ O I L ■ M I A
N E E ■ E I D E R S ■ T E R R
N S C ■ N O U N ■ A V A S T
■ R A I N[CAT]S A N D[DOG]S
G E E S E ■ O L A V ■ U S D
T R E K ■ D E R I V E ■ R O O
O A K ■ S O X ■ I N T E R N
■[DOG][CAT]C H E R S T R U C K
T W E E T ■ A L I T ■ E P E E
N O V A E ■ L A N A ■ A T R Y
T O E R R ■ E N G R ■ T O Y S
```

17

```
T H R U ■ S I C K A S A D O G
W E E P ■ A T A N Y P R I C E
A L A S ■ N A T U R A L G A S
S P R I N G L E T ■ D E A L T
■ ■ Z E R O S ■ Y E N T A S
A S S I S I ■ T O R E ■ ■
S A I N T A L B A N S ■ T W O
H U N G ■ O I L ■ M O O N
E L K ■ P R I N C E H A R R Y
■ ■ F A U N ■ V E R T E X
S P L I N T ■ F L E A S ■
T I A R A ■ P A I N T B A L L
O P T I C N E R V E ■ A L I A
O P E N H O U S E S ■ R O A D
L A R G E P R I N T ■ S P R Y
```

18

```
R E N T A C A R ■ F L A W E D
O V E R R I C E ■ I O D I N E
N O B I G G I E ■ G U A R D S
A L B S ■ A D D E N D ■ E W E
L V I ■ A R R I V E ■ S T I R
D E S K S ■ A N E W ■ H A S T
■ S H I N D I G ■ T A U P E S
■ ■ T E R N ■ W O R T ■
C A S T R O ■ C A N D I C E
R A K E ■ P R O S ■ E N E R O
I M A N ■ S I M I A N ■ L A D
C I T ■ S H T E T L ■ S E S E
K L E P T O ■ S Y L L A B U S
E N R O O T ■ T O A S T E R S
T E S L A S ■ O U T T O S E A
```

19

```
B A S H ■ C A B S ■ A D H O C
E L I A ■ O R E O ■ D R A W S
D E L I ■ F R E D ■ D O N N A
S E L L S F O R A S O N G ■
■ ■ S L E W ■ U N E A S Y
■ A R T I E ■ A P E S ■ R O I
S W O O N ■ A R I D ■ S O U P
C H A N G E S O N E S T U N E
R I D E ■ L A S T ■ W A N D S
A R T ■ D U P E ■ W A R D S ■
P L O W E D ■ P E R T ■ ■
■ F A C E S T H E M U S I C
C R A V E ■ H O O D ■ R U S H
H E M E N ■ A N N E ■ N I L E
E X E R T ■ D Y E D ■ S T E W
```

20

```
C B S ■ C R O C ■ M A L A W I
R E A ■ H A L L ■ E D I T E D
I C U ■ U S D A ■ S H A M E S
N O N E T H E W I S E R ■ ■
G O A T E E ■ ■ C U R ■ S E W
E L S A ■ S O M E P E O P L E
■ ■ A T N O ■ S N E A K S
A I M E R ■ A I L ■ T R Y S T
C R I S C O ■ S E E S ■ ■
M O S T W A N T E D ■ D U A L
E N T ■ E R A ■ U G A N D A
■ ■ A L L Y O U C A N E A T
U P S I D E ■ G N A T ■ A G E
S T A R E S ■ L I T E ■ S E N
S A T Y R S ■ E X E S ■ E S S
```

21

```
M A H I   P A L E S   B A T S
A S I F   O F A R T   E D I E
B I G F A T L Y R E   A L A P
  H I D   L O N   M I R A
  C H E M I C A L C Y M B A L
F L O R I D A   H E E
O A R   T O R C H   A U D I S
R I S E   S T R U M   P E N A
E M E N D   A T B A T   C D I
  T O M   B R O I L E D
Q U A R T E R B A C K S A X
U N C A   N E O   E A R
A S O N   S T O L E N B A S S
D A R C   C R E O N   E N T O
S Y N E   H O D A D   L T R S
```

22

```
M A R C   S H E L V E   W W W
O L E O   M U D E E L   I R E
H I N D U U T O P I A   L Y E
S I D E S   U N N A M E D
  I S U Z U U S E D C A R S
A R T   R O M P   D S T
M O I   P L A S M   O M E N
I D O L   A S T O R   R O T E
D E N Y   S A R A H   N O W
  N B A   T A T A   A N T
F O N D U U T E N S I L S
E S T E L L E   K I T E S
T O E   O A H U U K U L E L E
E L S   V I E N N A   A R I A
S E T   A T E O U T   C Y S T
```

23

```
D E T R O I T M I C H I G A N
I T S A F R E E C O U N T R Y
M A K E A M E N T A L N O T E
E L S   N A S   U S C   S E T
        E S T E S
A S T   S T A N   H A I M
C H A R L O T T E B R O N T E
T A K E I T O R L E A V E I T
A C E U P O N E S S L E E V E
S K I P   E A S E   L E D
  S K E D S
A M I   I N E   B A M   A S U
S A T E L L I T E S T A T E S
A T E E N A G E R I N L O V E
S T A R S I N O N E S E Y E S
```

24

```
B R U T   F E T A   C L I V E
R O P E   E T O N   L I T E R
A T T N   A U C T I O N E E R
G E O D E S I C   S T E M S
  N E X T   A L O H A
A B O R T S   T O L E R A N T
P A G E R   B A R D S   P I A
P R O R A T E   R E H I R E S
L O O   V A L S E   O N I C E
E N D T A B L E   B R A C E R
  A G A I N   E S T O
  B E H A R   D E S E R T E D
P A L I N D R O M E   I P S O
F R A N Z   O F I T   C I T E
C E L I A   E F T S   E T E S
```

25

```
R O C K   I N L E T   A B L E
U G L I   B O O T H   S L U G
B R O N Z E S T A R   T U N A
Y E T   E R E   L I P R E A D
      M L I   L E A R
P A G O D A S   S L A Y I N G
I L O N A   M I T E R   B O L
P O L K   F A D E D   A B O U
E N D   A A R O N   S H O N E
D E M E R I T   O C T A N E S
  E M I R   O R B
R E D C A P S   D R U   P S I
A L A E   L O V I N G C U P S
M I L E   A D O R E   O P A L
P A S S   Y A W E D   Z A N E
```

26

```
A I N T ■ P L E A ■ A D M A N
S N O O T I E S T ■ R A I S E
T H E K I N G S T O N T R I O
R E V E L S ■ ■ ■ P I E ■ ■ ■
I R I S ■ ■ S P R E E ■ A R T
D E L ■ P E A L E D ■ A C I D
■ ■ ■ C A T N A P ■ E T H O S
■ T H E R A J Q U A R T E T ■
F R O N T ■ O U T M A N ■ ■ ■
E A S T ■ I S E E I T ■ N I A
E Y E ■ A M E S S ■ G E N S ■
■ ■ E I N ■ ■ ■ D R E A D S ■
T H E T R O U T Q U I N T E T
W A S T E ■ R A R E B R E E D
A L T A R ■ N E S T ■ E R D A
```

27

```
F E T E ■ A B O V E ■ A M A T
U L A N ■ C U B I T ■ V A R Y
J A C Q U E L I N E ■ I R O N
I L I U M ■ K E Y ■ S A L M A
■ ■ T I P ■ ■ L A O T I A N ■
H O U R ■ I N D ■ M O O N S ■
A W R Y ■ B O U V I E R ■ ■ ■
L E N ■ K E N N E D Y ■ S T U
■ ■ O N A S S I S ■ H M O S ■
■ R O R E M ■ T N T ■ E O N S
S A D D E S T ■ ■ ■ S L O ■ ■
A I D E S ■ W P A ■ R I T T S
U S M A ■ P I L L B O X H A T
D I A L ■ O X I D E ■ E L S A
I N N S ■ S T E A L ■ S Y S T
```

28

```
L A B S ■ I N S ■ S E A C O W
O L E O ■ H O P ■ N E V A D A
G L A U C O M A ■ I R O N E D
J U M P U P A N D D O W N ■ ■
A R E S T ■ D I R E ■ I M P ■
M E D ■ ■ O I S E ■ I B A R ■
■ ■ M A R C H I N P L A C E ■
A S L O P E ■ ■ O A K L E Y ■
F L A P B O T H A R M S ■ ■ ■
R O W E ■ ■ M E N D ■ A F L ■
O W N ■ T E A T ■ C A L L A ■
■ S I M O N D I D N T S A Y ■
G O A W A Y ■ S W A N L A K E
P O L I T E ■ E A T ■ A C E R
O P E N E D ■ T R A ■ S E S S
```

29

```
B A N K G U A R D ■ A L E R T
O N O N E S W A Y ■ A I M E E
B O N E H E A D S ■ A B A B A
S N E E R ■ Y I P ■ C R I E R
■ ■ A L I T ■ O H R E A L L Y
A N T I G E N ■ E E L S ■ ■ ■
M O A N ■ N O R M A L ■ M I L
B E L G ■ S T O I C ■ C E D E
I L L ■ H I T E S T ■ H M O S
■ ■ R O T H ■ M E L R O S E ■
N Y A H N Y A H ■ D O O R ■ ■
B O G I E ■ T O M ■ S M A S H
O W E N S ■ B U I L T I N T O
M I N O T ■ A R T S T U D I O
B E T S Y ■ D I T T O M A R K
```

30

```
J I L L S T J O H N ■ E D A M
O R E O C O O K I E ■ C O P E
C O T T O N E D T O ■ H O P I
K N I T T E D ■ ■ S P O R E S
E S T ■ T R I P P ■ A I M A T
Y O G A ■ S M A L L S C A L E
S N O B S ■ A N A C T ■ T S R
■ ■ S H A G G Y D O G ■ ■ ■ ■
T A E ■ A L G A E ■ R E W E T
H I G H F L I E R S ■ E R N E
E R G O T ■ O A S T S ■ I C E
A C R O S S ■ ■ C R O P T O P
T O O K ■ P U L L I N H E R E
R O L E ■ A N O U K A I M E E
E L L Y ■ N U M B E R L E S S
```

31

S	T	O	R	E		E	S	A	U		S	O	A	R
T	R	A	I	L		C	H	I	N		Y	U	L	E
O	U	T	O	F	D	O	O	R	S		R	T	E	S
W	E	S	T		O	N	R	Y	E		I	O	T	A
			E	P	C	O	T		N	O	N	F	A	T
P	O	O	D	L	E		L	E	T	S	G	O		
E	M	U		E	N	C	Y	C		M	E	R	C	I
R	A	T		A	T	A		R	I	O		D	A	D
T	R	O	T	S		P	O	U	T	S		E	R	E
	F	E	E	D	E	R		S	I	E	R	R	A	
I	M	P	E	D	E		B	L	E	S	S			
T	A	R	P		S	T	I	L	L		P	A	C	S
E	R	I	E		O	U	T	O	F	S	I	G	H	T
M	I	N	E		T	R	E	S		E	E	R	I	E
S	O	T	S		O	K	R	A		A	D	A	P	T

32

S	A	H	I	B		O	P	E	R	A		B	A	R
A	M	I	N	O		W	A	L	T	S		O	N	O
P	I	C	K	Y	P	I	C	K	E	T		N	I	B
			C	E	N	T	S		A	U	N	T	Y	
R	A	P	S	O	N	G	S		L	I	B	Y	A	N
E	R	U	P	T	S			C	A	R	I	B		
S	T	P	A	T		B	O	O	Z	E		O	O	F
T	O	P	S		S	A	R	G	E		E	N	T	R
S	O	Y		B	A	R	B	S		P	E	N	T	A
		P	U	L	S	E			H	I	R	E	O	N
T	A	U	R	U	S		A	N	A	L	Y	T	I	C
A	P	P	L	E		E	R	O	D	E				
L	A	P		J	U	N	K	Y	J	U	N	K	E	T
I	R	E		A	N	G	I	E		P	I	A	N	O
A	T	T		Y	A	R	N	S		S	A	N	D	Y

33

D	O	B	R	O		T	R	O	D		Z	A	P	S
I	S	L	E	T		R	O	L	E		A	M	I	E
P	L	A	N	E		O	P	E	C		G	I	L	L
S	O	H	E	L	P	M	E	G	O	D		N	O	M
		G	L	O	P		D	A	K	O	T	A		
W	E	R	E	O	V	E	R	H	E	R	E			
A	L	I			E	A	S	I	N	E	S	S		
I	L	O	V	E		A	N	T		N	O	L	I	E
L	A	T	I	T	U	D	E				I	L	L	
	T	H	R	O	W	T	H	E	B	A	L	L		
M	O	S	A	I	C			A	U	E	R			
O	U	I		C	H	E	C	K	P	L	E	A	S	E
R	I	T	A		I	R	A	E		I	N	I	N	K
A	J	A	R		N	O	T	I		E	D	D	I	E
L	A	R	K		S	O	O	N		R	A	S	P	S

34

B	O	L	O		J	A	G	S		S	T	A	L	L
A	V	I	A		U	S	E	S		A	N	N	I	E
J	E	F	F	E	R	S	O	N		V	O	I	L	A
A	R	T		P	I	E		J	E	T	T	A	S	
		W	H	E	N	Y	O	U	R	E	A	C	H	
S	R	T	A		S	T	E	A	L					
W	E	A	V	E		T	H	E	E	N	D	O	F	
A	L	B	E	R	T	A		U	P	S	T	A	T	E
Y	O	U	R	R	O	P	E		S	E	T	I	N	
		O	S	A	K	A		S	A	S	S			
T	I	E	A	K	N	O	T	I	N	I	T			
E	V	A	D	E	S		N	C	R		A	H	A	
P	A	G	A	N		A	N	D	H	A	N	G	O	N
I	N	E	P	T		P	O	L	O		B	E	L	T
D	A	R	T	S		E	V	E	R		A	D	D	S

35

F	B	I	F	I	L	E		T	A	B	A	S	C	O
R	E	C	R	O	O	M		O	N	E	S	T	O	P
A	T	E	I	N	T	O		P	A	L	E	A	L	E
G	O	B		A	T	T	E	S	T		A	N	O	N
I	K	E	A		S	E	A	T			D	R	T	
L	E	E	R	S		D	R	O	P		A	T	T	O
E	N	R	O	O	T		T	R	U	E	L	O	V	E
		M	U	R	P	H	Y	B	E	D				
O	N	S	A	L	E	A	T		S	K	I	B	I	B
L	O	P	S		E	N	O	S		S	N	I	D	E
D	C	I			G	N	U	S		E	R	S	T	
P	O	N	D		S	L	E	E	P	S		D	A	W
R	U	N	U	P	T	O		D	E	A	D	E	Y	E
O	N	E	R	O	U	S		E	N	D	O	R	S	E
S	T	R	A	I	N	S		S	T	E	T	S	O	N

36

```
C A C T U S   A S K S F O R
O N L I N E   C R E A T I V E
U G A N D A   L I T T E R E D
P L U S E S   A S I T W E R E
L E D E R H O S E N   A B L E
E D E L W E I S S   P R O A M
    A L L Y   T O D A Y S
    R A T T L Y   H O I S T S
M E L E E S   V E I N
A M B E R   T E L L T A L E S
F I A T   R E S P E C T I V E
I N C I D E N T   T O O L E D
O D O M E T E R   T U N I N G
S E R E N I T Y   E N C A S E
O R E S T E S   S T E N O S
```

37

```
W A L K S   A B E L   N A T S
I N E R T   C L I O   I N I T
S T E A L   C A N O P E N E R
P I C K U P T H E P A C E
  S H A K E S     L E M O N
    T E N   B A W L   E R E
E S S O   S E R G E I   A B S
P U T A F I R E U N D E R I T
S I R   R O D E N T   V A T S
O T O   O N E D   A L I
M E N D S     A P O L L O
  G E T T H E L E A D O U T
C U B B Y H O L E   T O R T E
S P O T   O M A R   H E A R S
I N X S   R E N T   E R N E S
```

38

```
O A H U   G O O P   D A R N S
O L A N   A C R E   E L I O T
M I D D L E E A R   P L A T A
P B S   A L A N   L O O S E N
H I T C H I N G P O S T
  L O C   L Y E S O A P
A D E E R   S H E A   M N O
C O F F E E T A B L E B O O K
E S T   L A T E   L O O N Y
D E S P A I R   A D S
  E N T R A N C E H A L L
M I L L I E   T E C S   W O O
A R I L S   F R E E T R A D E
R A R E E   A I D S   O R E S
K E A T S   B A S S   T E N S
```

39

```
G S A   P A S T S   A D L E R
O H S   O C T A L   M I A T A
B I P   D H A B I   P S Y C H
A R C H I E B U N K E R
D R A M A     G I R A F F E
  S T O O P   P E E R I N
A B U   R O D E O   L A N A
B E T T Y F O R D C L I N I C
A T I E   M O O L A   C S T
C O L L I E   T R I B E
K N E E C A P     R E G A L
  V E R O N I C A L A K E
A D L I B   G O M A D   V I N
L A S S O   O R O N O   E T O
I N D E X   S A N E R   L A X
```

40

```
G L O B E   A S E A   T E A
R A N A T   D E A L   M O N T
O V E R A N D O U T   O A T H
  A R C   F L U   A U N T I E
  T O E   C E L   I N T E R N
S O U L   S S E   F R E E S
A R N O L D   O N C U E
S Y D N E Y A U S T R A L I A
  A N E S T   A L L O T S
G R O S S   P H D   C O C K
R A S P E D   K I T   A K A
E N C A S E   O N O   N I N
E S A I   C A R G O P A N T S
C O R N   O G E E   A D O B E
E M S   Y E A R   M A N E T
```

41

```
ALPS  JIMI  ITWAS
SIRE  AVIS  DWELT
IBID  VETO  EERIE
NEVADA  LEARNER
IRANI  TADA  PENN
NAT  SPINETS  REL
ELEPHANT  DONKEY
  PARTYANIMAL
MORTAR  CAREBEAR
AVA  GOTINTO  MCA
CECE  NADA  NAPES
ARTLESS  BERETS
BRIMS  SAVE  ORAL
RACES  EGAD  METE
ENERO  LENS  ARES
```

42

```
SATE  MENOFSTRAW
CLOG  AREWETHERE
AGOG  TABLELINEN
MAKELESS  ONEAD
  ADORE  DOUSERS
GATORS  CURIE
OMANI  RARESTEAK
BOX  TENAM  ACE
SKIMPEDON  CASTE
  AERIE  CAVEIN
COPLAND  TONIO
ADIOS  GOMADFOR
PIEDATERRE  FURY
OUTONALIMB  ASEA
SMARTMONEY  NEON
```

43

```
TARO  ASTA  BABAS
ODOR  DAIS  AMIGO
NASA  OMNI  YODEL
SMALLPOTATOES
  ATA  HUB
AWARDS  TOE  ASST
CONED  MANIA  HIE
TRIVIALPURSUITS
ORS  ERIES  SPRAT
RYES  GIS  RISERS
  TOO  AES
 PETTYOFFICERS
ADULT  ANTE  AVOW
TULLE  LEER  LIMA
MOLAR  ERRS  FLAT
```

44

```
ERIC  LILAC  AMEN
DADO  ABOIL  PILE
THOMASMORE  ASIS
  BUTS  AORTAS
OBLIGE  DONATE
LEANED  RUST  RTE
DATER  MATES  CEL
ITIS  JAPES  CHAD
EEN  HUGER  RAISE
SNL  AMOR  HARPER
 OLDBOY  ODISTS
NAVAJO  ARIL
ALEC  JOHNMILTON
SERE  ELATE  OKIE
HESS  TAMIL  NOLO
```

45

```
NARC  MILE  BAITS
ADIA  AMES  APNEA
BOG[USA]LIBIS  SLANG
 ALINE  OHS[USA]NNA
AFT  AMAJ  DOVEIN
COOL  ATEST  ERS
TUNEIN  ROVER
ILIAD  [USA][USA][USA]  PAWNS
 VIGIL  TAGOUT
 SSE  AREAS  ERLE
THO[USA]ND  MRED  KLM
RECLUSE  OLIOS
ARIOT  YO[USA]IDWHAT
SPANS  RELO  LOPE
HALEY  ERST  SPED
```

46

```
ACRE  SPUD  ACTOR
DIEU  TERI  CHORE
DISCREDIT  IRMAS
   THEWICKEDITCH
WHERES  HAN  SILO
BODED    DOTTED
APO  ATATIME
 INTERNREVENUE
  WARTIME   NRA
MARINE    WALDO
ODOR AOL  SHRIEK
 DOLLARSTONUTS
ERLES  OCCIPITAL
LEERY  LOAD  EERO
TERSE  ELSE  RDAS
```

47

```
CHOCOLATECOATED
AEROBICEXERCISE
CAPTIVEAUDIENCE
HRH SETTLES  CAP
ESAS SORTS  TAPE
TANEY NOS  LINEN
SYSTOLES  TENSED
    TUBS EENY
METERS  STRATEGO
ALIEN MIA  SIREN
SALS SINGS  META
CPL CONCEAL  MEL
ASANALTERNATIVE
REGISTEREDVOTER
ADELAIDESLAMENT
```

48

```
MANTRAPS  SKIMPS
IVEHADIT  ONHIRE
NOSECONE  RIOTED
INTHERED  ESPOSA
OLEO NAMATH  SIT
NERTS LASH  CIDE
SASSED  NEUROSES
   EARS  AMOR
LISALOEB  BARCAR
UNIT MALI  NEHRU
MEL LEMONS  LAMS
BRIGID  WHOCARES
ARCANA  PALATINE
GOOVER  OLIVEOIL
ORNERY  PEDESTAL
```

49

```
BEECH  SALT  ISAK
ADLAI  OREO  ACRE
YUMMYYUMMY  GRAD
   PAAR  SCRUBS
ACTS NODS  HEMS
THAI KNEEDEEP
RUSTS  STYE  TIA
INTEARS  HEROINE
AGE HAHA  SNOUT
 STAGEMOM  TURN
 AGAR ASIA  ASEA
AORTAS  LAIR
GLEE MMMMMMGOOD
REAR OBOE  PEDRO
ARTS GAIN  STEER
```

50

```
EAGLE  CAMP  RANK
MORON  AWOL  ODIE
BRANDONAME  MANY
ETS GREY  THAMES
RASCALS  SHIN
   AMY PHOTOOPS
PASTE HAIR  FLAT
AUTO BERRA  OGLE
CRAB EAST  GRASP
TABULATE  SOU
   RICH CLAMSUP
LENGTH GOAL  PRO
IDOL BONOVOYAGE
AGRA URAL  NOTES
REAR MEWS  GUSSY
```

51

```
C O R E A   S T A T     S K I N
O R A L S   L I V E     L A N E
N I P A T   I D E A     O N T O
J O I N I N M A R R I A G E
O L E     E E L     S N A R L
B E R A T E S   A F T   R I O
    L A D   O D E   W O O F
W E W O U L D F O R S H O R T
E X I T   E A T   T I E
L P S   D D S   D I R E C T S
L E T M E     P A L   A H A
  D A Y B E F O R E T H U R S
E I R E   T A L K   O A S I S
S T I R   N I K E   A L E V E
S E A S   A L A N   D O S E D
```

52

```
R I F E   P R A T T     B R A N
E N O S   R I C H E     I O N A
E R R S   O C E A N S T A T E
V O T E S F O R W O M E N
E A R N S       S R A
D D E   T Y K E     R A C E R
  S U S A N B A N T H O N Y
M A S C   D O O N E   M U S E
A M E L I A B L O O M E R
H A S A T   A N N A   T N T
    A T F     U S H E R
  J U L I A W A R D H O W E
P H O N O G R A P H   R U M P
H E L D   R A D I O   E S A I
I N T O   E D E N S   W E N D
```

53

```
P E R C H E S   S T A B L E D
O N A L A R K   C R A Y O L A
M C G U I R E   H A N O V E R
E Y E B R O W   O L D B E A N
    C C L   S O A P
M A G O O   H E L L   N A P S
I C O U L D E A T A H O R S E
C O R P O R A T E L A D D E R
R O G E R O V E R A N D O U T
O L E S   P E R M   G I R D S
    F A N S   M O N
A N N U A L S   N O U G A T S
B E A S T I E   E S T O N I A
C A P E A N N   S H A F T E D
S T A R L E T   S E T F I R E
```

54

```
M E C H   S H E A F   D R U B
O L I O   H E L G A   V E N A
M E A T M A R K E T   O T I S
A V O C A D O   R E W R I T E
  H Y E N A   L I A R
S A H I B S   T R I N K E T S
A T A L E   S T A N D   M R I
V A N I L L A I C E C R E A M
E R G   L O I R E   H O N D O
D I S C I P L E   L I S T E N
  H O N E   S L I M S
T H E R E A T   O N E E Y E D
H E A T   R H I N E S T O N E
E A V E   E A T E N   T U T U
O R Y X   D I O R S   I D O S
```

55

```
H A U L   I R I S H   C H I A
A S T A   T A B O O   L O O N
S T I C K S H I F T   U P T O
N I C E L Y   A R A B I A N
T R A D E   A C R O S S
    E C R U   D I O N N E
L I M B   H O E S   A D I O S
A R I A   O S C A R   A T I T
R A N T S   E A S T   S E R E
A N I M A L   R H E A
    O N E I D A   C R E M E
S O Y B E A N   S N A R E S
A L A I   P A D D L E B O A T
G I R L   E N T R E   I D L E
A N N E   R E S E W   N E S S
```

56

```
F O A L   ▓ C U B S ▓ O N S E T
O M N I   ▓ A S A P ▓ V E R N E
L E T O   ▓ M E R E ▓ E R O D E
K N I T T E D S C A R F ▓ ▓ ▓ ▓
▓ ▓ T I L ▓ ▓ S C H ▓ T H O ▓ ▓
C O C A C O L A ▓ H E A R O F ▓
A L L ▓ T I M B E R W O L F ▓ ▓
R E E F S ▓ M B A ▓ E L U D E ▓
B A R R E L B O L T ▓ P E R ▓ ▓
O R I O L E ▓ Y I E L D E R S ▓
N Y C ▓ E A R ▓ E A U ▓ ▓ ▓ ▓ ▓
▓ ▓ I N H A L I N G F O O D ▓ ▓
H I N D I ▓ J E N A ▓ F O U R ▓
A D I E U ▓ A G O G ▓ E Z R A ▓
S A L E M ▓ H O N E ▓ L E S T ▓
```

57

```
I N L A W ▓ A L F A ▓ ▓ P O L E
N O O S E ▓ B O R E ▓ ▓ R H E A
F E L T I N O N E S B O N E S ▓
O L L A ▓ E D G E ▓ ▓ I V O R Y
▓ ▓ R O H E ▓ L U K E ▓ ▓ ▓ ▓ ▓
J U S T D I S C O V E R E D ▓ ▓
O S T E O ▓ A V E ▓ ▓ B R E D ▓
H U A ▓ M A C L E A N ▓ ▓ A T E
N A T S ▓ R A E ▓ ▓ E P S O M ▓
▓ L E T T E R B E F O R E X I ▓
▓ R A S P ▓ L I N O ▓ ▓ ▓ ▓ ▓ ▓
S T R A W ▓ O D I N ▓ P O P S ▓
C R O S S W O R D S T A P L E ▓
A I L S ▓ E L I E ▓ O N E A L ▓
M O L E ▓ T S P S ▓ M E S T A ▓
```

58

```
M A T ▓ O L O F ▓ ▓ A P R O N
A T E ▓ S A M O A ▓ L O O N Y
R O N ▓ S I N G L E P L A C E
I N A M E R I C A W H E R E ▓
S E M I ▓ ▓ I D E A S ▓ ▓ ▓ ▓
▓ ▓ N I P A T ▓ ▓ I S I S ▓ ▓
B E A U T Y C O N T E S T ▓ ▓
N O R ▓ I P O ▓ A N O ▓ W H Y
T H E A M A Z I N M E T S ▓ ▓
H O W L ▓ ▓ S T Y L E ▓ ▓ ▓ ▓
▓ L A V A L ▓ ▓ R Y E S ▓ ▓ ▓
▓ F O U R S T A T E S M E E T
F O U R C O R N E R S ▓ A L A
R A Z E D ▓ A D M I T ▓ S E C
I L O S E ▓ S A C S ▓ T R Y ▓
```

59

```
A R C H ▓ B A T T E R ▓ G A P
M A L E ▓ U R S U L A ▓ A V A
A G E D ▓ S E A B I S C U I T
S T A G ▓ H A R M ▓ H O G A N
S I N E W Y ▓ S A C ▓ M U T E
E M E R I T I ▓ N A P P I E S
D E R ▓ T A B S ▓ T R E N D S
▓ ▓ W H I M S I C A L ▓ ▓ ▓ ▓
R A C H E L ▓ A S H Y ▓ D A S
A D H E R E S ▓ M A E W E S T
D U A L ▓ D A H ▓ F R A P P E
I L I A D ▓ T A P E ▓ S L I P
C A N N E R Y R O W ▓ T O R I
A T E ▓ L O R E N Z ▓ E R I N
L E D ▓ L O S S E S ▓ D E N S
```

60

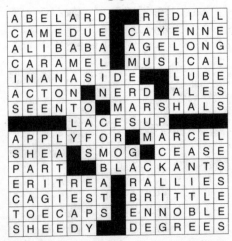

```
A B E L A R D ▓ R E D I A L
C A M E D U E ▓ C A Y E N N E
A L I B A B A ▓ A G E L O N G
C A R A M E L ▓ M U S I C A L
I N A N A S I D E ▓ L U B E
A C T O N ▓ N E R D ▓ A L E S
S E E N T O ▓ M A R S H A L S
▓ ▓ ▓ L A C E S U P ▓ ▓ ▓ ▓
A P P L Y F O R ▓ M A R C E L
S H E A ▓ S M O G ▓ C E A S E
P A R T ▓ B L A C K A N T S
E R I T R E A ▓ R A L L I E S
C A G I E S T ▓ B R I T T L E
T O E C A P S ▓ E N N O B L E
S H E E D Y ▓ D E G R E E S
```

61

```
STEPSON   THELOOP
TAXRATE   NICEONE
EXPECTANTMOTHER
RILE  ETE     SLOT
IWON  ROWDY   LAVE
LADE    BOA   ILES
EYED  BRONX   PART
      LEROI
PATH  AUNTS   LEAR
ASEA  INB     AXLE
TINS  READS   LIDO
ESTD    BAP   AGER
LABORDAYWEEKEND
LIENORS   ENTENTE
ADDEDUP   STARTER
```

62

```
SONIC   HOLM   IRES
ERICH   ERIE   NOAH
WAKEISLAND   NAVE
ORE  SCI  TAPERED
NESTEA   TYLER
   ELLER   SOCKET
DOWN   DRAW   NINAS
IRON   SOFAS   ROSA
SCRIP  OFAN   CBER
KANSAS   ICALL
   CYNIC   PAELLA
DEPOSIT   OAR  AIM
ESAU   PAWNTICKET
STIR   ELEE   ARENO
KENT   RYES   TORSO
```

63

```
ONAN   BING   BYFAR
NOMO   ISEE   EARLY
ALIT   GARR   SMOTE
ITSNOTYOUITSME
RESOLE   NOB
   WENEEDTOTALK
LPS  STAG   AYEAYE
EROS   RAG   ERLE
NOFUSS   DAMN   PEP
IWANTMYSPACE
   DOA   DALLAS
   WEVEGROWNAPART
BACON   RHEE   ACNE
ECOLI   ONES   SEAN
DONTS   WOKS   ORZO
```

64

```
BLOT   CALMS   MOTH
BECK   UBOAT   ECHO
KATTSPAUSE   THEN
INASNIT   SWOOSH
NOV  EDER   NOTUP
GNOME   REACT   ALP
   IZE   DWI   ELKS
   BAERSCLAUSE
SPYS   MOO   OPT
NOR   PAWAT   SHAWL
OLDIE   TREE   PHI
   ESPRIT   ONTOPOF
NCAA   CROWESFEAT
PAYS   BUYER   FAME
RTES   MELLO   SLID
```

65

```
IMOFF      CANVAS
RADIAN    CONCERT
IVERSON   LASORDA
SETSTHEPACE   HEN
  NOTWITHIT   FONZ
  POTTER   PLENA
  MERTON   REEVES
  HARKEN   MINXES
CAUSER   JUSTIN
ARDOR   BELOIT
TMAN   HADITMADE
TOD   MINISTERIAL
INAPOKE   HONIARA
SIMILES   STALLS
HASPED   ONSET
```

66

M	O	N	T	E	Z	U	M	A		S	C	U	B	A
A	N	Y	D	A	Y	N	O	W		K	A	Z	O	O
C	O	N	S	U	M	I	N	G		I	N	I	N	K
A	N	E			U	N	K	E	M	P	T			
W	E	X	F	O	R	D		E	M	P	I	R	E	S
			L	U	G	E	R		D	E	L	A	N	O
A	P	T	E	R	Y	X	E	S		D	E	V	O	N
R	E	H	E	M		E	S	O		O	V	E	T	A
A	N	I	T	A		D	E	L	I	V	E	R	E	R
B	I	S	O	N	S		T	O	N	E	R			
S	N	I	F	F	L	E		P	A	R	S	E	C	S
			F	L	Y	L	E	A	F			C	O	P
O	T	T	O	I		M	A	R	L	S	T	O	N	E
S	E	W	O	N		E	S	T	A	T	E	L	A	W
S	C	O	T	T		R	E	S	T	R	A	I	N	S

67

P	L	O	P		N	C	O		A	P	P	L	E
R	I	P	A		K	O	O	L		G	L	E	A	M
E	S	A	U		L	E	A	D		R	E	L	I	T
P	A	L	L	M	A	L	L		Z	E	A	L		
		V	A	T	S		L	E	E		G	T	O
R	A	P	I	D	S		A	N	D	I	R	O	N
E	M	I		A	C	T	O	R		R	A	M	S
P	O	L	L	T	H	E	A	U	D	I	E	N	C	E
E	E	L	S		S	T	E	A	D		T	A	T
A	B	O	U	N	D	S		B	E	A	S	T	S
L	A	W		A	A	A		T	B	A	R		
	T	R	I	M		P	U	L	L	O	V	E	R
A	V	A	I	L		N	U	D	E		M	A	Y	O
W	I	L	D	E		I	Z	O	D		A	M	E	X
L	A	K	E	R		T	O	R		S	P	R	Y

68

P	E	Z		E	D	G	Y		P	O	W	W	O	W
E	C	O		T	A	L	E		I	D	O	I	D	O
C	H	O	W	C	H	O	W		T	E	R	R	O	R
S	O	S	A		L	A	S	S			S	E	R	F
		C	H	I	T		E	L	S	E
	T	A	K	E	A	S	O	L	E	M	N	V	O	W
B	O	S	O	X		W	I	N	E		A	N	A
A	R	K		A	M	O	N	G	S	T		S	L	R
T	S	E		G	O	R	E			A	S	C	O	T
H	O	W	N	O	W	B	R	O	W	N	C	O	W
		A	N	N	E		B	E	A	R
M	A	I	M		D	A	L	I		U	F	O	S
A	S	S	E	S	S		H	I	G	H	B	R	O	W
S	T	A	I	R	S		A	G	H	A		E	P	A
K	O	W	T	O	W		B	E	T	H		E	S	P

69

C	R	I	S	P		D	A	H	L		T	A	D	S
S	A	N	T	A		A	R	E	A		O	R	E	L
A	N	T	E	C	E	D	E	N	T		W	I	L	E
		H	E	S	T	O	N		E	M	I	G	R	E
O	P	E	D		D	E	A	L	W	I	T	H	I	T
O	A	T		L	S	D		V	O	N		T	O	Y
P	L	U	T	O			D	I	R	G	E			
		B	E	T	T	E	M	I	D	L	E	R
		K	U	R	T	Z				E	L	A	N	D
G	R	R		S	A	C		W	A	D		I	C	E
R	A	I	S	E	S	H	E	E	P		S	N	O	W
A	M	B	U	S	H		L	A	P	S	E	D		
S	P	A	R		C	A	L	L	T	O	A	R	M	S
S	E	L	F		A	L	I	T		F	L	O	O	R
O	D	D	S		N	A	S	H		T	Y	P	E	A

70

B	E	T	H		S	A	C	K			S	A	R	A
A	R	I	E		A	S	H	E		A	C	N	E	D
HA	R	R	Y	C	HA	P	I	N		M	A	N	S	E
I	S	O	B	A	R		C	O	M	P	L	E	T	E
			A	D	A	M		A	L	P	HA			
C	O	M	B	S		T	R	I	K	E		T	S	E
O	K	A	Y		S	E	I	N	E	S		HA	U	L
S	I	R		T	HA	T	S	T	HA	T		W	A	D
M	E	T		O	R	N	E	R	Y		R	A	V	E
O	S	HA		S	P	A	N	O		L	A	Y	E	R
		G	A	T	E		S	C	O	W				
A	I	R	L	A	N	E	S		O	N	D	E	C	K
S	T	A	I	D		C	HA	R	L	I	E	C	HA	N
I	T	HA	C	A		O	N	E	D		A	H	M	E
S	O	M	E		L	E	S	S		L	O	P	E	

71

D	E	A	D	S	P	O	T	■	P	H	E	L	P	S
R	A	D	I	A	L	L	Y	■	O	O	L	A	L	A
A	R	I	S	T	I	D	E	■	K	U	D	R	O	W
G	L	O	R	I	E	S	■	B	I	S	E	C	T	S
■	■	S	O	N	S	■	T	U	N	E	R	■	■	■
A	R	A	B	Y	■	K	I	N	G	S	■	M	T	V
S	E	M	I	■	S	E	E	I	F	I	C	A	R	E
T	H	I	N	K	I	N	G	O	U	T	L	O	U	D
R	A	G	G	E	D	Y	A	N	N	■	E	T	N	A
A	B	O	■	R	E	A	M	S	■	M	A	S	K	S
■	■	B	O	R	N	E	■	F	I	N	E	■	■	■
A	R	I	O	S	O	S	■	B	O	R	S	T	A	L
L	A	B	R	E	A	■	A	I	R	R	O	U	T	E
I	S	L	A	N	D	■	R	E	C	O	U	N	T	S
A	P	E	X	E	S	■	I	N	E	R	T	G	A	S

72

F	O	O	T	R	U	B	■	C	B	R	A	D	I	O
I	M	P	R	O	V	E	■	I	L	O	V	E	L	A
L	I	E	A	B	E	D	■	V	O	T	E	F	O	R
M	G	R	■	B	A	L	T	I	C	■	S	I	C	S
S	O	A	R	■	S	A	H	L	■	■	C	A	M	■
E	S	T	E	S	■	M	A	L	E	■	L	I	N	E
T	H	E	G	A	P	■	T	A	R	G	E	T	O	N
■	■	■	G	L	A	S	S	W	A	R	E	■	■	■
O	N	P	A	T	R	O	L	■	S	E	R	A	P	E
N	O	S	E	■	T	H	I	S	■	G	A	M	A	Y
A	M	A	■	E	F	T	S	■	■	T	E	L	E	■
L	I	N	D	■	S	L	E	E	P	S	■	M	A	W
E	N	D	E	D	U	P	■	R	U	L	E	O	N	E
R	E	Q	U	I	E	M	■	E	R	O	T	I	C	A
T	E	S	T	A	T	E	■	S	N	E	E	R	E	R

73

S	A	I	L	■	E	L	E	V	■	L	O	G	A	N
M	U	L	E	■	L	O	B	E	■	I	V	A	N	A
E	L	L	A	■	D	E	A	N	■	V	A	L	E	T
L	A	I	D	D	O	W	N	T	H	E	L	A	W	■
T	I	N	■	E	R	E	■	I	A	N	■	■	■	■
S	T	I	G	M	A	■	O	L	D	■	W	E	A	K
■	■	■	E	U	D	O	R	A	■	H	O	R	D	E
P	O	W	E	R	O	F	A	T	T	O	R	N	E	Y
A	N	I	S	E	■	F	L	E	E	T	S	■	■	■
N	O	N	E	■	C	C	S	■	A	T	E	A	S	E
■	■	■	A	P	E	■	D	R	U	■	M	T	A	■
■	C	O	P	S	A	N	D	R	O	B	B	E	R	S
L	O	P	E	S	■	T	O	E	S	■	A	L	I	T
O	C	A	L	A	■	E	D	G	E	■	R	I	P	E
S	A	L	T	Y	■	R	O	S	S	■	B	A	E	R

74

C	O	M	A	■	T	B	I	L	L	■	B	L	A	B
A	D	A	M	■	O	L	L	I	E	■	L	O	S	E
T	I	N	A	L	O	U	I	S	E	■	A	N	T	E
S	E	X	■	O	T	R	A	■	■	I	D	E	A	S
■	■	■	B	O	B	D	E	N	V	E	R	■	■	■
B	O	O	H	O	O	■	■	R	I	I	S	■	■	■
E	L	I	A	■	■	C	E	A	S	E	■	B	A	A
G	I	L	L	I	G	A	N	S	I	S	L	A	N	D
S	O	Y	■	M	A	R	G	E	■	■	O	L	D	E
■	■	■	M	A	R	T	■	■	P	A	N	D	A	S
■	■	J	I	M	B	A	C	K	U	S	■	■	■	■
F	A	U	N	S	■	■	L	E	S	E	■	A	A	A
I	M	I	N	■	A	L	A	N	H	A	L	E	J	R
T	A	C	O	■	H	O	R	D	E	■	A	R	A	T
S	T	E	W	■	S	T	O	O	D	■	D	O	R	Y

75

A	L	F	A	■	E	L	B	O	W	■	S	H	A	M
T	A	R	S	■	R	E	E	C	E	■	H	A	T	E
K	N	E	W	■	N	I	G	H	T	C	O	U	R	T
A	D	E	A	L	■	S	I	R	■	A	R	T	I	E
■	M	A	N	O	F	■	N	E	W	S	T	E	P	S
Z	I	G	■	P	E	N	N	■	E	E	L	■	■	■
O	N	E	R	■	R	O	I	L	S	■	I	F	S	O
L	E	N	A	■	R	U	N	A	T	■	S	O	N	S
A	S	T	I	■	A	N	G	I	E	■	T	O	O	L
■	■	N	C	R	■	O	R	N	O	■	T	W	O	■
M	I	S	C	H	I	E	F	■	D	R	I	F	T	■
O	M	A	H	A	■	C	F	O	■	G	R	A	I	L
W	A	T	E	R	G	L	A	S	S	■	A	U	R	A
E	R	I	C	■	S	A	L	S	A	■	N	L	E	R
R	I	N	K	■	A	T	L	A	S	■	I	T	S	A

The New York Times

Crossword Puzzles

The #1 name in crosswords

Available at your local bookstore or online at nytimes.com/nytstore

Coming Soon!

Supersized Book of Weekday Crosswords	0-312-37042-3	$15.95/$19.95 Can.
Will Shortz Presents Fun in the Sun Crossword Puzzles Omnibus	0-312-37041-5	$11.95/$14.95 Can.
How to Conquer The New York Times Crossword Puzzle	0-312-36554-3	$9.95/$11.95 Can.
Crosswords Under the Covers	0-312-37044-X	$6.95/$8.50 Can.
Afternoon Delight Crosswords	0-312-37071-7	$6.95/$8.50 Can.
Favorite Day Crosswords: Tuesday	0-312-37072-5	$6.95/$8.50 Can.
Crosswords for a Mental Edge	0-312-37069-5	$6.95/$8.50 Can.

Special Editions

Brainbuilder Crosswords	0-312-35276-X	$6.95/$8.50 Can.
Fitness for the Mind Crosswords Vol. 2	0-312-35278-6	$10.95/$13.50 Can.
Vocabulary Power Crosswords	0-312-35199-2	$10.95/$13.50 Can.
Will Shortz Xtreme Xwords Puzzles	0-312-35203-4	$6.95/$8.50 Can.
Will Shortz's Greatest Hits	0-312-34242-X	$8.95/$10.95 Can.
Super Sunday Crosswords	0-312-33115-0	$10.95/$13.50 Can.
Will Shortz's Funniest Crosswords Vol. 2	0-312-33960-7	$9.95/$11.95 Can.
Will Shortz's Funniest Crosswords	0-312-32489-8	$9.95/$11.95 Can.
Will Shortz's Sunday Favorites	0-312-32488-X	$9.95/$11.95 Can.
Crosswords for a Brain Workout	0-312-32610-6	$6.95/$8.50 Can.
Crosswords to Boost Your Brainpower	0-312-32033-7	$6.95/$8.50 Can.
Crossword All-Stars	0-312-31004-8	$9.95/$11.95 Can.
Will Shortz's Favorites	0-312-30613-X	$9.95/$11.95 Can.
Ultimate Omnibus	0-312-31622-4	$17.95/$21.95 Can.

Daily Crosswords

Daily Crossword Puzzles Vol. 72	0-312-35260-3	$9.95/$11.95 Can.
Fitness for the Mind Vol. 1	0-312-34955-6	$10.95/$13.50 Can.
Crosswords for the Weekend	0-312-34332-9	$9.95/$11.95 Can.
Monday through Friday Vol. 2	0-312-31459-0	$9.95/$11.95 Can.
Monday through Friday	0-312-30058-1	$9.95/$11.95 Can.
Daily Crosswords Vol. 71	0-312-34858-4	$9.95/$11.95 Can.
Daily Crosswords Vol. 70	0-312-34239-X	$9.95/$11.95 Can.
Daily Crosswords Vol. 69	0-312-33956-9	$9.95/$11.95 Can.
Daily Crosswords Vol. 68	0-312-33434-6	$9.95/$11.95 Can.
Daily Crosswords Vol. 67	0-312-32437-5	$9.95/$11.95 Can.
Daily Crosswords Vol. 66	0-312-32436-7	$9.95/$11.95 Can.
Daily Crosswords Vol. 65	0-312-32034-5	$9.95/$11.95 Can.
Daily Crosswords Vol. 64	0-312-31458-2	$9.95/$11.95 Can.
Volumes 57-63 also available		

Easy Crosswords

Easy Crossword Puzzles Vol. 7	0-312-35261-1	$9.95/$11.95 Can.
Easy Crosswords Vol. 6	0-312-33957-7	$10.95/$13.50 Can.
Easy Crosswords Vol. 5	0-312-32438-3	$9.95/$11.95 Can.
Volumes 2-4 also available		

Tough Crosswords

Tough Crosswords Vol. 13	0-312-34240-3	$10.95/$13.50 Can.
Tough Crosswords Vol. 12	0-312-32442-1	$10.95/$13.50 Can.
Tough Crosswords Vol. 11	0-312-31456-6	$10.95/$13.50 Can.
Volumes 9-10 also available		

Sunday Crosswords

Sunday Brunch Crossword Puzzles	0-312-36557-8	$6.95/$8.50 Can.
Everyday Sunday	0-312-36106-8	$6.95/$8.50 Can.
Sunday Puzzle Omnibus Vol. 32	0-312-36066-5	$9.95/$11.95 Can.
Sunday Morning Crossword Puzzles	0-312-35672-2	$6.95/$8.50 Can.
Sunday in the Park Crosswords	0-312-35197-6	$6.95/$8.50 Can.
Sunday Crosswords Vol. 30	0-312-33538-5	$9.95/$11.95 Can.
Sunday Crosswords Vol. 29	0-312-32038-8	$9.95/$11.95 Can.

Large-Print Crosswords

Large-Print Crosswords for Your Bedside	0-312-34245-4	$10.95/$13.50 Can.
Large-Print Will Shortz's Favorite Crosswords	0-312-33959-3	$10.95/$13.50 Can.
Large-Print Big Book of Easy Crosswords	0-312-33958-5	$12.95/$15.95 Can.
Large-Print Big Book of Holiday Crosswords	0-312-33092-8	$12.95/$15.95 Can.
Large-Print Crosswords for Your Coffeebreak	0-312-33109-6	$10.95/$13.50 Can.
Large-Print Crosswords for a Brain Workout	0-312-32612-2	$10.95/$13.50 Can.
Large Print Crosswords to Boost Your Brainpower	0-312-32037-X	$11.95/$14.95 Can.

Large-Print Easy Omnibus	0-312-32439-1	$12.95/$15.95 Can.
Large-Print Daily Crosswords Vol. 2	0-312-33111-8	$10.95/$13.50 Can.
Large-Print Daily Crosswords	0-312-31457-4	$10.95/$13.50 Can.
Large-Print Omnibus Vol. 6	0-312-34861-4	$12.95/$15.95 Can.
Large-Print Omnibus Vol. 5	0-312-32036-1	$12.95/$15.95 Can.
Previous volumes also available		

Omnibus

Crosswords for a Long Weekend	0-312-36560-8	$11.95/$14.95 Can.
Crosswords for a Relaxing Vacation	0-312-36696-7	$11.95/$14.95 Can.
Holiday Cheer Crossword Puzzles	0-312-36126-2	$11.95/$14.95 Can.
Supersized Sunday Crosswords	0-312-36122-X	$16.95/$21.00 Can.
Biggest Beach Crossword Omnibus	0-312-35667-6	$11.95/$14.95 Can.
Weekend Away Crossword Puzzle Omnibus	0-312-35669-2	$11.95/$14.95 Can.
Weekend at Home Crossword Puzzle Omnibus	0-312-35670-6	$11.95/$14.95 Can.
Sunday Crossword Omnibus Volume 9	0-312-35666-8	$11.95/$14.95 Can.
Lazy Sunday Crossword Puzzle Omnibus	0-312-35279-4	$11.95/$14.95 Can.
Supersized Book of Easy Crosswords	0-312-35277-8	$14.95/$18.50 Can.
Crosswords for a Weekend Getaway	0-312-35198-4	$11.95/$14.95 Can.
Crossword Challenge	0-312-33951-8	$12.95/$15.95 Can.
Giant Book of Holiday Crosswords	0-312-34927-0	$11.95/$14.95 Can.
Big Book of Holiday Crosswords	0-312-33533-4	$11.95/$14.95 Can.
Tough Omnibus Vol. 1	0-312-32441-3	$11.95/$14.95 Can.
Easy Omnibus Vol. 5	0-312-36123-8	$11.95/$14.95 Can.
Easy Omnibus Vol. 4	0-312-34859-2	$11.95/$14.95 Can.
Easy Omnibus Vol. 3	0-312-33537-7	$11.95/$14.95 Can.
Easy Omnibus Vol. 2	0-312-32035-3	$11.95/$14.95 Can.
Daily Omnibus Vol. 16	0-312-36104-1	$11.95/$14.95 Can.
Daily Omnibus Vol. 15	0-312-34856-8	$11.95/$14.95 Can.
Daily Omnibus Vol. 14	0-312-33534-2	$11.95/$14.95 Can.
Sunday Omnibus Vol. 8	0-312-32440-5	$11.95/$14.95 Can.
Sunday Omnibus Vol. 7	0-312-30950-3	$11.95/$14.95 Can.
Sunday Omnibus Vol. 6	0-312-28913-8	$11.95/$14.95 Can.

Variety Puzzles

Acrostic Puzzles Vol. 10	0-312-34853-3	$9.95/$11.95 Can.
Acrostic Puzzles Vol. 9	0-312-30949-X	$9.95/$11.95 Can.
Sunday Variety Puzzles	0-312-30059-X	$9.95/$11.95 Can.
Previous volumes also available		

Portable Size Format

Expand Your Mind Crosswords	0-312-36553-5	$6.95/$8.50 Can.
After Dinner Crosswords	0-312-36559-4	$6.95/$8.50 Can.
Crosswrods in the Sun	0-312-36555-1	$6.95/$8.50 Can.
Will Shortz Presents Crosswords To Go	0-312-36694-9	$9.95/$11.95 Can.
Favorite Day Crosswords: Monday	0-312-36556-X	$6.95/$8.50 Can.
Piece of Cake Crosswords	0-312-36124-6	$6.95/$8.50 Can.
Carefree Crosswords	0-312-36102-5	$6.95/$8.50 Can.
Groovy Crosswords from the '60s	0-312-36103-3	$6.95/$8.50 Can.
Little Black (and White) Book of Crosswords	0-312-36105-X	$12.95/$15.95 Can.
Will Shortz Present Crosswords for 365 Days	0-312-36121-1	$9.95/$11.95 Can.
Easy Crossword Puzzles for Lazy Hazy Crazy Days	0-312-35671-4	$6.95/$8.50 Can.
Backyard Crossword Puzzles	0-312-35668-4	$6.95/$8.50 Can.
Fast and Easy Crossword Puzzles	0-312-35629-3	$6.95/$8.50 Can.
Crosswords for Your Lunch Hour	0-312-34857-6	$6.95/$8.50 Can.
Café Crosswords	0-312-34854-1	$6.95/$8.50 Can.
Easy as Pie Crosswords	0-312-34331-0	$6.95/$8.50 Can.
More Quick Crosswords	0-312-34246-2	$6.95/$8.50 Can.
Crosswords to Soothe Your Soul	0-312-34244-6	$6.95/$8.50 Can.
Beach Blanket Crosswords	0-312-34250-0	$6.95/$8.50 Can.
Simply Sunday Crosswords	0-312-34243-8	$6.95/$8.50 Can.
Crosswords for a Rainy Day	0-312-33952-6	$6.95/$8.50 Can.
Crosswords for Stress Relief	0-312-33953-4	$6.95/$8.50 Can.
Crosswords to Beat the Clock	0-312-33954-2	$6.95/$8.50 Can.
Quick Crosswords	0-312-33114-2	$6.95/$8.50 Can.
More Sun, Sand and Crosswords	0-312-33112-6	$6.95/$8.50 Can.
Planes, Trains and Crosswords	0-312-33113-4	$6.95/$8.50 Can.
Cup of Tea and Crosswords	0-312-32435-9	$6.95/$8.50 Can.
Other volumes also available		

For Young Solvers

New York Times on the Web Crosswords for Teens	0-312-28911-1	$6.95/$8.50 Can.
Outrageous Crossword Puzzles and Word Games for Kids	0-312-28915-1	$6.95/$8.50 Can.
More Outrageous Crossword Puzzles for Kids	0-312-30062-X	$6.95/$8.50 Can.

St. Martin's Griffin